100 PART-TIME JOBS FOR MOTHERS

100
PART
TIME
JOBS
FOR
MOTHERS

Christine Green

**KOGAN
PAGE**

First published in 1991

Kogan Page Limited
120 Pentonville Road
London N1 9JN

British Library Cataloguing in Publication Data

A CIP record for this book is available from the British Library.

ISBN 0-7494-0178-8

Typeset by DP Photosetting, Aylesbury, Bucks
Printed and bound in Great Britain by
Clays Ltd, St Ives plc

Contents

Introduction

Women are gaining an increasingly important position in the workplace as the number of young people preparing to enter the job market continues to decline. No one understands this better than the government which is busily creating schemes designed to attract a largely untapped workforce back to work. Women are being offered the opportunity to learn brand new skills or to brush up on old ones.

Many women are unable to work full time because of family commitments, but part-time work has many advantages to offer: it can supplement the family income, broaden horizons, improve confidence through increased independence, and even supply a taster for full-time work later on. It should come as no surprise to learn, then, that 82 per cent of part-time workers are women and that the numbers are growing fast.

In principle, most jobs can be worked on a part-time basis, but it should be stressed that the majority of jobs organised in this way carry less responsibility and are thus of lower status than full-time positions. As work patterns begin to change employers are starting to realise the advantages of taking on part-timers. Indeed, a random survey of over 40 UK companies recently found that most employers believed that part-time workers were the answer to their firms' skill shortages.

Some employers offer a warm welcome to staff wishing to return to work on a part-time basis, provided that they have kept in touch with the latest developments, attending re-training sessions when required. Professional women, in particular, are inclined to do this without being told and are thus better equipped than most to explore and identify work opportunities for themselves. Job sharing, where two or more share the responsibilities and status of a full-time job, is mainly catching on in the professional area.

Employers, too, are well aware of the need to keep part-time staff happy and may devise strategies to do just that. Boots, for instance, which is a large employer, is currently operating a scheme, soon to become nationwide, offering working mothers opportunities for term-time only employment. During the school holidays the jobs are taken over by students. More than half the workforce at Marks and Spencer's are part time, and B & Q is more than happy to arrange hours to suit the domestic responsibilities of its part-time staff.

But what are the chances of work for someone who has never had a job, has no qualifications, or who is not as young as she was? To that we would answer that every woman has something to offer an employer whatever her age, although it becomes trickier after 55. Years spent running a home and rearing a family should be regarded as valuable work, requiring as it does a number of complex managerial skills, as well as the ability to retain one's identify at the same time.

The qualifications mentioned are those obtainable today, but equivalents are usually acceptable. For example, GCSE (General Certificate of Secondary Education) has replaced GCE O level and CSE.

Finding a job may seem an impossible task with present levels of unemployment, but it should be remembered that not everyone is looking for part-time work. It is hoped that *100 Part-Time Jobs for Mothers* will give readers an insight into the many opportunities that exist for part-time workers and will encourage women to go out to seek them.

The material in the book is organised in such a way that someone interested in becoming, say, a Care Assistant, can turn to that particular entry for a brief job description, rates of pay, skills required, and a short analysis of the job's requirements, together with the qualifications needed, if any. Also, where appropriate, information is given on promotion prospects, and there's a useful section relating to suggested jobs in similar fields. *Women looking for part-time work should go first to the local press and the Job Centre.* Organisations listed at the end of entries and on page 151 will provide additional information.

Accounting Technician

Hours	Several days per week
Pay	Full-time accounting technicians can earn £9000–£16,000 but this depends on experience
Personal qualities	Numerate; quick; accurate; neat; honest; methodical; able to work alone or as member of team

An accounting technician is responsible for gathering together the financial information which is required by the accountant. The main areas in which she may be employed are: industry, local government and public practice.

Her duties will vary in each area but if employed in a local authority she may prepare the accounts, calculate the salaries and wages, collect overdue payments, pay creditors and also deal with customers.

In public practice she will generally assist the chief accountant in preparing and checking the accounts; she could possibly become involved with other more complex aspects such as trusteeship, and receivership.

In industry or commerce her duties vary enormously. In the smaller company she may undertake a wide range of accounting duties and in a larger organisation concentrate specifically on one particular area.

An accounting technician will generally work under the supervision of a qualified accountant; she may work alone or as part of a team within an accounting department.

Qualifications and experience
Accounting technicians must first register as student members of the Association of Accounting Technicians (AAT) in order to study for the full membership examinations. These courses are held: part-time/full-time/day release/or by correspondence at various polytechnics and colleges. Part-time entails three years of study, while full-time takes two years.

Candidates require four GCSE passes (A–C) in subjects including English and maths/statistics and only one craft.

Mature students aged 21 years and over, without the required qualifications, may still study for the AAT examinations, provided they possess a GCSE pass (A–C) in English, or display a good understanding of English and a numeracy subject. Exemption from various parts of the examinations may be permitted for candidates who have worked in accountancy. After the age of 30 opportunities for entry diminish.

The BTEC runs a course with the AAT, which can be taken instead of the AAT course.

Other jobs
Accounts Clerk; Bank Clerk

Contact
Specialist publications in which vacancies appear: *Financial Weekly, Local Government Chronicle, Management Accounting, Accountancy, Accountant, Accounting Technician, Opportunities* (for local government vacancies)

Write to: The Development Officer (Communications), Association of Accounting Technicians, 154 Clerkenwell Road, London EC1R 5AD; 071-837 8600

Acupuncturist

Hours	Sessional work several hours per week
Pay	£5–£20 per session
Personal qualities	Sympathetic; patient; scientifically minded; tactful; accurate

Acupuncture is based on a very old Chinese theory that there are two flows of energy within the human body, Yin and Yang, and that basically good health relies on a balance of both.

An acupuncturist treats patients by inserting needles into various parts of the body therefore curtailing pain, curing illness or causing anaesthesia.

Before treatment can begin she examines the patient, and discusses in detail his or her past medical health. From this information she can make a diagnosis of the problem and prescribe the relevant treatment which could involve the patient attending fortnightly or monthly sessions. Some acupuncture is practised by doctors working in the NHS, but most is done privately.

Each particular area of alternative medicine offers its own training programme. Colleges offer a variety of courses, each with its own entry requirements. Costs can be around £1500 for a year's course.

Qualifications and experience
Mature students are welcomed by all the alternative therapies, but it is important to contact individual colleges to establish their required entry qualifications.

For candidates who possess a qualification in medicine or one of the other alternative therapies, The British College of Acupuncture, in association with the British Acupuncture Association and Register offers part-time courses. After one year students are awarded the Diploma in Acupuncture (DIPAc); after two years the Licentiate (LicAc); after four years the Bachelor of Acupuncture (BAc); and finally, after six years, Doctor of Acupuncture (DrAc).

The International College of Oriental Medicine requires applicants to be aged between 23 and 50 years; possess two A levels and three GCSE passes (A–C) including chemistry/ physics and human biology/biology.

The full-time three-year course is followed by a fourth year part-time course which leads to the Bachelor of Acupuncture. After three years a limited licence to practise is awarded. At the end of the fourth and final year the BAc qualification replaces it.

To gain entry on to the three-year part-time course at the College of Traditional Chinese Acupuncture students need A levels. During the first two years of the course students work at home with monthly weekend attendance at college for practical and theory instruction.

Third year students are assigned two weeks' practical experience in a clinic, followed by six weeks of attending college one day a week where they diagnose and treat patients. After successfully completing the examinations students are then permitted to practise, but are supervised for a further six months. At this point a licentiate is awarded.

Other jobs
Chiropodist; Medical Herbalist; Homoeopath; Osteopath; Naturopath

Contact
Write to: The Institute for Complementary Medicine, 21 Portland Place, London W1N 3AF; 071-636 9543

London School of Acupuncture & Traditional Chinese Medicine, 3rd floor, 36–7 Featherstone Street, London EC1Y 8QX; 071-490 0513

British College of Acupuncture, 8 Hunter Street, London WC1N 1BN; 071-833 8164

International College of Oriental Medicine, Green Hedges House, Green Hedges Avenue, East Grinstead, Sussex RH19 1DZ; 0342 313106

Alteration Hand

Hours	Flexible
Pay	£2.50 per hour
Personal qualities	Good eyesight; neat and meticulous; reliable; conscientious; able to work under pressure

A store selling curtains, a dress shop, a bridal store, or a dry cleaning shop may offer the services of an alteration hand. This is someone employed to undertake any repairs or alterations to customers' garments, which may involve mending a broken zip, taking in or letting out a garment, making curtains, or simply adjusting the hem of a dress or coat.

In large stores an alteration hand may work on the premises; a smaller shop may use an outworker; occasionally clothing manufacturers require the services of an experienced worker to do some hand sewing.

It is possible, and indeed quite popular, for women who already own the necessary equipment to set up their own alteration business and work from home.

Qualifications and experience
Although no general academic qualifications are required such a job really does call for experience, either working in a factory as a machinist, or as a dressmaker/tailor.

Other jobs
Sewing Machinist; Tailoress/Dressmaker; Cutter

Contact
Place your own advertisement

Applications Programmer

Hours	Freelances can often determine their own hours
Pay	Freelance programmers can earn up to £2000 per month but this depends very much on experience
Personal qualities	Logical; patient; creative; good communicator; numerate; dependable; able to work alone or as member of team

An applications programmer is responsible for preparing programs which will, in turn, instruct the computer to carry out certain tasks. She takes a logical look at the company's requirements and then devises a program to deal with them. She also tests the program and eliminates any faults. Jobs are becoming more difficult to get.

Qualifications and experience
Mature entrants who have had experience working with computers are looked upon favourably. It is important that all applicants have a good understanding of computer systems.

Many large companies organise in-house training and some will accept candidates with two A levels or the equivalent on to their training programme.

Holders of degrees in any subject may enter programming. Degree courses in computer science are available to students with A levels, a degree or the equivalent. Content of courses varies so it is wise to check this before applying. The courses best suited to application programmers are those which include some business/commercial subjects. Entry on to a degree course is usually a minimum of two A levels plus three GCSE passes (A–C).

The BTEC Higher National course in computing studies and other subjects is widely available. The course is studied on a part-time basis and takes two to three years. Entry requirements: one A level plus three GCSE passes (A–C).

Full-time college courses offer qualifications regarded as equivalent to A levels and some offer practical experience. The courses are: BTEC National Certificate, City & Guilds Certificate and the National Computing Centre (NCC) Threshold Certificate.

It is still possible for candidates with no academic qualifications to gain employment.

The British Computer Society organises examinations for those already employed in computer work. Entry requirements: one A level plus four GCSE passes (A–C) including English and maths and also 12 months' practical experience in computing. Another examination is set by the Institute of Data Processing Management. Entry requirements: four GCSE passes (A–C) including English and maths. This is usually undertaken on a part-time, day release, evening class or correspondence course basis.

It is quite possible for computer operators to progress to programming, and study for qualifications part-time.

Other jobs
VDU Operator

Contact
Specialist publications: *Computing; Computer Weekly; Data Processing; Computer Talk; Datalink* for vacancies

Write to: National Computing Centre, Bracken House, Charles Street, Manchester M1 7BD; 061-228 6333

British Computer Society, 13 Mansfield Street, London W1M 0BP; 071-637 0471

Assembly Worker

Hours	Shift work could be 4pm–9pm or 8pm–12pm. Depends on the company but there are usually vacancies on various shifts
Pay	After training and experience to build up speed an assembler can earn from £85 to £169 per week
Personal qualities	Accurate; neat; able to work as member of team; able to follow instructions; methodical; patient

The manufacturing industry employs a great many part-time workers and one of the most popular areas is on the assembly line.

Assembly workers are usually involved in the making up of products such as washing machines, video recorders or other

17

household electrical appliances. This may involve attaching small components such as pins or washers to the item as it passes along on a conveyor belt. Alternatively, partially completed items may be brought over to the assembler's place of work where she will affix the various components before sending them on to the next stage of their development.

Often the work requires the assembler to follow a set of detailed instructions and she may need to use an assortment of tools such as screwdrivers, pliers or soldering irons.

New recruits attend a short training programme, in which they will be shown how to read diagrams and be taught other special techniques. Otherwise, training is on the job under the supervision of an experienced worker.

Assembly work can be exhausting, especially when standing or sitting in the same position throughout the shift.

Qualifications and experience
Mature applicants are generally looked upon favourably in this area of employment where personal attributes are far more important than academic qualifications. Many employers set an aptitude test for candidates especially when the work is the assembly of small components which demand great accuracy.

It is usual for recruits to possess a good standard of general education with GCSE passes in English or maths. Experience in needlework and other practical subjects can also be very useful.

Other jobs
Checkout Operator; Dry Cleaning/Laundry Worker; Cutter

Contact
Write to local firms which may have vacancies for shift workers

Audio/Copy Typist

Hours	Depends on the employer. Much temporary work is available, especially during the summer holidays
Pay	£3.50 per hour; up to £3.75 for audio
Personal qualities	Accurate; methodical; tidy; neat; quick; versatile; able to work on own or as part of team. An audio typist must be able to listen and follow instructions

Offices create a great many jobs for women who would like to return to work on a part-time basis and typing is one area in which there are always vacancies.

An audio typist transcribes cassettes or tapes which are played back on a dictating machine through headphones; she operates the machine by foot controls. She checks the work when it is complete. An audio typist often combines her job with other routine tasks. A copy typist generally works from handwritten drafts, producing letters, reports, minutes, invoices and a wide range of material. She also makes masters or stencils for duplicating or photocopying machines.

If the typist is employed in a typing pool, her work is usually checked by a supervisor but if working alone she checks the work herself.

In a large organisation a copy typist with training and experience can become a supervisor.

Qualifications and experience
Employers usually expect staff to have a good standard of education and preferably some GCSE passes (A–C), including maths and English; also to have taken a typing course and/or to have followed this up with a course at a commercial college learning basic office skills and improving typing ability. Prospects are good for mature applicants who possess relevant office experience.

College courses in commercial and secretarial subjects generally lead to recognised qualifications awarded by var-

19

ious examining bodies. Many employers encourage their employees to improve their skills and qualifications by allowing them part-time or day release to attend courses at colleges of further education. In some parts of the country there may be job training schemes for adults.

Other jobs
Word Processor Operator; Filing Clerk; Telex/Fax Operator; Secretary; Clerk

Contact
Secretarial agencies

Audiology Technician

Hours	Several days per week
Pay	The nationally agreed pay scale for technicians employed by the NHS ranges from £5510 to £12,000
Personal qualities	Patient; methodical; able to speak clearly; able to put people at ease; able to work as part of team

An audiology technician tests the hearing ability of adults and children using specialist instruments, and is able to determine the degree of impairment and so prescribe appropriate hearing aids. She also prepares individually moulded hearing aid ear inserts; alters them to fit the patient and then instructs the patient on their use.

She is generally employed in an out-patients' clinic within an ear, nose and throat hospital. Vacancies exist within the education authority for audiology technicians to work solely with children.

Qualifications and experience
There is no age limit so mature applicants, especially those with experience in engineering/electronics, are considered for training.

Most student audiology technicians work under the supervision of senior medical staff and attend a day release/block release course, leading to the BTEC National Certificate in Medical Physics and Physiological Measurement.

Most employers expect their staff to possess four GCSE passes (A-C) including science subjects, or alternatively two A levels, again including a science subject.

The British Society of Audiology runs a two-year course for audiology technicians. Although training is done on the job, students undertake an examination set by the Society.

Other jobs
Laboratory Technician; Medical Photographer

Contact
Specialist publications in which vacancies appear: *Nature*, *New Scientist*

Write to: British Society of Audiology, c/o Audiology Department, Royal National Throat, Nose and Ear Hospital, 330 Gray's Inn Road, London WC1X 8DA; 071-837 8855

Bank Clerk

Hours	Dependent on the branch's requirements
Pay	Approximately £4–£6 per hour
Personal qualities	Honest; smart; pleasant; polite; numerate; good communicator

In theory there is no job within the bank that cannot be undertaken on a part-time basis. Many banks are now operating a re-entry scheme for married women wishing to return to work.

During their time away from the bank these women are required to work a certain number of days, perhaps covering holidays and sick leave, and must attend refresher courses.

Qualifications and experience

It is rare for a mature applicant to be accepted into the world of banking without experience, because of the lengthy training programme that has to be followed. But if you have had experience working perhaps as a building society clerk or for any other financial establishment you should have little trouble in finding employment.

Other jobs

Building Society Clerk; Clerk; Bookkeeper; Receptionist

Contact

The Personnel Department at banks

Bar Staff

Hours	Mainly shift work either mornings, lunchtimes or evenings
Pay	Wages Council minimum basic rate: not less than £2.50 per hour for those aged 21 or over
Personal qualities	Pleasant; smart; polite; sociable; adept at mental arithmetic; honest

There are many opportunities for part-time bar staff: in hotels, restaurants, pubs, wine bars, leisure centre complexes, night clubs, on trains, ships and airports.

The job includes selling a wide range of drinks, perhaps cigarettes and sometimes food. It is important that bar staff are fully acquainted with the selection of drinks on sale, and, when asked, are able to mix the very latest cocktails.

Prior to the bar opening, staff must ensure that supplies are adequate, and everything is prepared for the customers. While on duty they must: dry up any bar spillages, wipe the tables, in some bars collect empty glasses, and serve bar meals. After closing time, bar staff usually stay behind to wash up the dirty glasses and cash up the money in the till.

Training is done on the job under the supervision of the publican or pub manager, and you will normally work alongside one or two other members of staff. The City & Guilds Specific Skills Scheme, Food and Beverage Service (707) and Bar Service (7005), is a nationally recognised qualification for those who want to learn more about bar work. The courses concentrate on practical skills. No qualifications are required for entry.

Qualifications and experience
No formal qualifications are required to work in a bar; however, there is a minimum age limit of 18 years. Bar work isn't easy. It involves standing for hours on end, trying to pacify awkward customers who claim they've been waiting a long time to be served, and the smoky, at times boisterous, environment is not congenial to everyone.

It can be an attractive job for someone who thrives on pressure, is a good listener and can remember faces and the favourite drinks of regular customers easily.

Other jobs
Waitress; Counter Service Assistant; Midday Supervisor

Beauty Therapist

Hours   Flexible. May be asked to work irregular
                               hours depending on the employer. Can also
                               operate on a self-employed basis

Pay	No national set standard. Payment depends on the employer but is usually compared with hairdressers' wages, ie about £83 per week after training, rising to over £100
Personal qualities	Physically fit; friendly; able to listen; interested in the human body; neat and tidy; if self-employed, ability to drive is useful

The aim of a beauty therapist is to make the client both feel, and look, good. She does this by administering beauty treatments and applying make-up to clients, and whenever the situation warrants, gives extra treatment such as wax baths, manicures and pedicures, toning up unused muscles, the removal of any unwanted hair by one of several methods in which training has been received. She may also deal with clients who have skin blemishes.

Most opportunities in beauty salons are full time, but there is always the possibility of freelancing, either visiting clients in their own homes or having them visit the therapist. This is an ideal situation and can work out well for a busy housewife.

Qualifications and experience

It is possible to find employment in beauty therapy without the recognised qualifications, but this is not recommended.

Entry requirements for courses vary, so it is necessary to check with colleges of further education before planning to enrol. Many private colleges also offer courses. Courses may be full time, day release or evening, and last from three months to three years; longer courses usually include hairdressing.

The City & Guilds Beauty Therapist Certificate (304) is a two-year full-time course and covers the full range of beauty treatments practised in beauty salons.

Confederation of Beauty Therapy and Cosmetology offers: Diploma/Certificate for Assistant Beautician, Diploma of Aestheticiennes, Diploma in Beauty Therapy, Diploma in Electrolysis. These courses are available in a few state colleges and also some private colleges. The entry requirement is three GCSEs (A–C).

International Health and Beauty Council (IHBC) offers:

International Beauty Therapist's Diploma, and an International Diploma in Health and Beauty Therapy. Entrance requirements are two A levels or five GCSEs or equivalent.

The International Therapy Examination Council (ITEC) offers qualifications in Beauty Therapy, Teacher Training (Beauty Therapy), Stage and Character Make-up etc. The minimum educational requirement is five GCSEs including English language and biology.

Although the actual content of courses may differ, they all cover a wide range of subjects including anatomy and physiology, cosmetic chemistry, health and hygiene, face and body massage, electrical treatments and depilation, make-up and cosmetics, manicure and pedicure, diet and nutrition.

Other jobs
Hairdresser; Retail Assistant

Contact
Write to: Confederation of Beauty Therapy and Cosmetology, 2nd Floor, 34 Imperial Square, Cheltenham G150 1QZ; send SAE; 0242 570284

International Therapy Examination Council, 16 Avenue Place, Harrogate, North Yorkshire, HG2 7PJ; 0423 880193

International Health and Beauty Council, 109a Felpham Road, Felpham, West Sussex PO22 7PW; 0243 860320

Bingo Caller

Hours	Typically three afternoons or three evenings a week, possibly Saturdays
Pay	Approximately £2.90 per hour
Personal qualities	Clear voice; pleasant; witty; smart

Bingo is a popular pastime enjoyed by thousands of men and

women up and down the country. The game is not only played in bingo halls, but also amusement arcades, hotels, and fun fairs.

The bingo caller usually controls the game. Her other responsibilities include: announcing the numbers as they are chosen by the machine or by hand and then transferring those numbers on to the marker board. When the game is over she will check the winning cards against the numbers on her board, check over the equipment before the game begins and occasionally she may be requested to sell the bingo cards.

Full training is given before starting the job.

Qualifications and experience
No formal qualifications are required to be a bingo caller; however, if you have had experience, you would obviously be at an advantage

Other jobs
Interviewer; School Crossing Patrol; Entertainer

Bookkeeper

Hours	May be several days a week depending on company or clients
Pay	£5–£6 per hour
Personal qualities	Neat handwriter; reliable; honest; accurate; patient; numerate

Bookkeepers are constantly in demand, especially by small businesses. They are employed to: balance the books, deal with invoices and receipts, take care of the wages, be fully conversant with VAT, National Insurance, PAYE, deal with the tax inspector, and generally prepare accounts in readiness for final checking by the accountant. Accountants are responsible for the preparation of clients' accounts, ensuring that they show a true picture of the company's overall financial status. It is a job which requires qualifications.

Many firms have computerised accounting systems but in those which are not yet fully automated, the pen, work sheet, and adding machine are very much in use.

Qualifications and experience
Experience in bookkeeping would be an advantage, but that is not to say an employer would not look favourably upon someone with the ability and a track record of office experience.

Although there are no specific qualifications most employers would expect their staff to have had a good general education with some GCSE passes in maths and English (A–C). Other useful subjects are typing, accounts and business studies.

Most training is done on the job alongside an experienced member of staff but some firms run short instruction classes.

Students with no academic qualifications may study for the BTEC General Certificate/Diploma. The Certificate involves one year part-time study and the Diploma is a two-year part-time course.

Other jobs
Checkout Operator; Retail Assistant; Clerk

Bookmaker Cashier

Hours	Approximately 25 hours per week
Pay	£12 per afternoon with additional payments when racing requires extra hours to be worked
Personal qualities	Pleasant; able to handle money confidently; reliable; trustworthy; smart; numerate

Bookmakers, turf accountants or bookies, as they are often called, offer odds and accept bets on the basis of sporting activities, mainly horse and dog racing.

Cashiers are employed to: take bets from members of the general public, record them, pay out winnings and also deal with the filing of bets, together with the general running of the betting office which usually includes marking up the boards displaying the races to be held.

Betting shops are generally open six days a week, with Saturday the busiest, and as there are many races held on bank holiday weekends, it is usual to work unsocial hours.

Because of the complexity of dealing with sums of money, which can be quite substantial at times, training is usually given on the job.

Qualifications and experience
No formal qualifications or experience in bookmaking are required. Many companies encourage their cashiers to learn the basics of the settlement of bets, and wherever possible, cashiers are given the opportunity of taking a short course.

Other jobs
Market Research Interviewer; Checkout Operator; Book-keeper

Building Society Cashier

Hours	Usually dependent on the requirements of the branch. It may entail working on Saturdays and filling in for cases of sickness or holidays
Pay	£2.50–£5 per hour but this usually depends on the building society, and experience of the applicant
Personal qualities	Pleasant; numerate; smart; polite; trustworthy; able to communicate; accurate

A building society cashier works in a branch office undertaking general clerical duties. She deals with customers wanting to make cash transactions, handles enquiries from members of the general public who come to the office, assists those who wish to open accounts and offers advice to investors on the benefits of various methods of saving. Depending on the size of the branch, the cashier may be responsible for answering the telephone and also dealing with correspondence.

Each building society organises its own training scheme but new recruits are usually trained on the job under the supervision of experienced staff. They may also attend courses at training centres run by either their employer or the Chartered Building Society Institute (CBSI).

Qualifications and experience
An employer would generally expect applicants to have a good standard of general education and possess at least four GCSE passes (A–C) including English and maths.

The applicant without the relevant academic qualifications who displays the necessary abilities and personal attributes may be accepted on merit. Mature applicants are similarly assessed; obviously it helps to have some commercial experience.

Other jobs
Receptionist; Bank Clerk; Bookkeeper

Contact
Building Societies Association, 3 Savile Row, London W1X 1AF; 071-437 0655

Chartered Building Society Institute (CBSI), 19 Baldock Street, Ware, Hertfordshire SG12 9DH; 0920 5051

Buyer

Hours	Depends on employer's requirements: those employed in the retail area may work several days per week
Pay	Average salaries for full-time buyers range between £6000 and £10,000 per annum. In senior positions, salaries range from £10,000–£13,000
Personal qualities	Good negotiator; methodical; numerate; responsible; decisive; well organised; able to get on with people

A buyer is responsible for ensuring that the company in which she is employed has sufficient supplies for their needs. This involves her establishing the company's requirements, seeking out the best source and then obtaining the goods at the best price. She also negotiates the terms and delivery dates, using her own judgement and skill.

In smaller organisations, a buyer may be responsible for purchasing everything from stationery to pieces of electronic equipment, while larger organisations may employ a number of buyers, each of whom concentrates on a different area.

Buyers are employed in various areas of industry, commerce, large hotels, catering outlets, and in the retail trade.

Most firms run their own training schemes. Many individuals with or without the relevant qualifications enter as trainee buyers, then progress to become assistant buyer and subsequently buyer. Those wishing to progress in this career study for the Institute of Purchasing and Supply (IPS) examinations run at one of over 100 colleges and polytechnics on a day release, part-time or evening class basis.

Qualifications and experience
Many firms welcome adult entrants as retail buyers provided they have had experience in a relevant area, ie marketing.

New entrants should preferably be: (a) aged 25 and under; possess two A levels and three GCSE passes (A–C) which should include English language and maths. BTEC awards are acceptable; (b) aged over 26 with sufficient experience in the retail trade, but without the above qualifications, who may be able to study for the IPS examinations. Further details are available from IPS. Other acceptable qualifications are a BTEC National Certificate or Diploma in Business Studies; (c) already working in purchasing, for whom the Association of Supervisors in Purchasing and Supply (ASPS) offers appropriate examinations. Entry requirements are: four GCSE passes (A-C), or two years' experience.

If candidates wish to become purchasing officers and members of the IPS, they must be over 26 with experience in a related area, ie marketing.

After gaining experience in the retail trade many people make a sideways move into buying. Larger organisations generally recruit their staff straight into buying, the minimum requirements being four GCSE passes (A-C).

Other jobs
Retail Work; Sales Merchandiser

Contact
Specialist publications in which vacancies appear: *The Institute of Purchasing and Supply Management Journal, The Management Services Journal, Materials Handling News*

Write to: The Institute of Purchasing and Supply and Association of Supervisors in Purchasing, Easton House, Easton on the Hill, Stamford, Lincolnshire PE9 3NZ; 0780 56777

Calligrapher

Hours	As long as it takes to do the job
Pay	Each job is priced separately; £30-£50 per job

Personal qualities	Neat handwriter; accurate; artistic; patient; reliable; able to work to deadlines

Calligraphy is the study and art of producing beautiful handwriting. Once regarded as an academic pursuit, calligraphy has slowly re-emerged in the commercial world and there is now a growing demand.

Opportunities exist for writing wedding invitations, church confirmation class awards, record company albums, general certificates, menus at top class restaurants. There is also an area for commissioned work in specialist maps and family tree chronicles, as well as for drawings to accompany botanical works.

Learn about the various styles practised through time, various pens, and writing material which were and are today used. Scour back copies of art journals and write to historical societies for any information they may have. The local library is a perfect source of information, and also a free one.

Qualifications and experience

A number of colleges offer evening classes in calligraphy and the local crafts council will be able to tell you where courses are being run in your area.

Once the basic skills have been mastered you are in a position to advertise. It may be as well to build up an extensive portfolio which can be shown to prospective clients.

Calligraphy can be a profitable sideline for someone who shows the ability and the talent.

Contact

Local crafts council; local library for further information

Write to: Association of Scribes and Illuminators, 54 Boileau Road, London SW13 9BL; 081-748 9951. Send SAE.

Care Assistant

Hours	Variable; there may be a requirement to work shifts
Pay	Differs according to employer and experience, with extra allowances for night duties. At the moment a full-time care assistant working in a day centre might earn £4000–£6000. Part-time remuneration is likely to be on a pro-rata basis.
Personal qualities	Genuinely interested in people; reliable; responsible; patient; tolerant; sympathetic; warm hearted

Care assistants are employed in a variety of establishments to provide care, offer support and also help to improve the quality of life for groups of people with differing needs.

They may work in residential homes, day centres, occasionally nurseries or schools, offering support where needed to single parents or homeless individuals who are going through a particularly difficult period.

Duties in various establishments will differ but include helping people dress and undress, assisting them when getting bathed, serving meals, helping them come to terms with their situation and encouraging them to be as independent as possible; assisting with recreational pursuits and escorting the people on outings when required.

If a care assistant is employed in a residential home, she may have to stay over the odd weekend.

Qualifications and experience
Maturity and experience are highly valued. Staff employed by the local authority or even those doing voluntary work may be encouraged to go on training courses.

The Certificate in Social Service awarded by the Central Council for Education and Training in Social Work (CCETSW) is a widely recognised qualification both in the National Health Service and also within many voluntary organisations. The basic principle of this training course is to expand on the skills and experience the applicant already possesses. Training lasts two to three years and involves attending college on a day/block release system or open learning. The Certificate in Social Service is gradually being replaced by the Diploma in Social Work. The training lasts for at least two years and the award is attainable at different levels: graduate, non-graduate and mature entrant.

BTEC First Certificate/Diploma in Caring (Caring and Community Services modules) are available at many colleges and last for one or two years of full-time study. Students are usually given work experience in a caring establishment where they are supervised.

The BTEC National Diploma in Social Care is a full-time two-year study course. Candidates require four GCSE (A-C) passes.

The City & Guilds (3251) Community Care Practice award has ben designed primarily for mature candidates who are employed in social care work or training for work in this area. No qualifications are required for entry and courses are widely available throughout the country. The Open College also offers the opportunity to sit for this qualification.

Other jobs
Nurse; Youth and Community Work; Nursing Auxiliary; Kitchen Assistant; Domestic Cleaner; Nanny; Home Help; Play Group Organiser

Contact
Write to: Central Council for Education and Training in Social Work; address on page 151

The National Council for Voluntary Organisations, 26 Bedford Square, London WC1B 3HU; 071-636 4066

Community Service Volunteers (The National Volunteer Agency), 237 Pentonville Road, London N1 9JN; 071-278 6601

Checkout Operator

Hours	May cover late night shopping and Saturdays
Pay	Wages Council minimum rate for those aged 21 or over not less than £2.48 per hour
Personal qualities	Pleasant; polite; smart; adept with figures; helpful

In most department stores and supermarkets it is customary for shoppers to serve themselves, taking the goods over to the checkout operator who will, in turn, check the goods through and take the money. The prices are entered, a total registered, and the operator takes payment from the customer, giving the correct change, which has usually been calculated by the till.

A checkout operator must also ensure that the service point is kept clean and well supplied with till rolls, plastic bags, pens, and the correct cheque card warning records.

As paying by cheque and credit card is common the checkout operator must know how to check that all the relevant details have been entered, a procedure taught during training.

Companies organise their own training schemes, some of which are conducted entirely by experienced staff. During such training sessions staff will be shown how to operate tills, what to do if the goods are unpriced, how to change till rolls, check cash cards and so on. It is quite usual for till operators to spend time working on the shop floor watching other experienced staff before starting themselves.

Qualifications and experience
Although in general no qualifications are required for this type of work, employers prefer applicants to have a good level of general education.

Other jobs
Retail Assistant; Counter Service Assistant; Cashier; Mer-

chandiser; Petrol Pump Attendant; Bookkeeper; Bookmaker
Cashier

Contact
Some larger supermarkets advertise vacancies within their
premises

Chiropodist

Hours	Two to three days per week if employed in NHS. Private practice chiropodists may work long, irregular hours
Pay	Salaries for full-time NHS chiropodists range from £7,335 rising to £16,075 according to various grades. Chiropodists employed privately are likely to earn more
Personal qualities	Patient; sympathetic; dextrous; tactful; self confident; happy to work alone; well organised

The job involves diagnosing and treating ailments of the feet,
which includes inspecting feet and deciding on the appropriate course of treatment. This could involve: massage, heat,
drugs, minor surgery, ultrasound etc, and occasionally a
chiropodist may have to perform minor skin and nail
operations under local anaesthetic. She also applies dressings, appliances, and ointments when required, and offers
counselling to patients on footwear.

Some pedicurists refer to themselves as chiropodists.
However, they are more properly in the beauty business,
doing for the feet what manicurists do for the hands.

Qualifications and experience
Mature students are welcomed into chiropody training

schools and some will waive their entry requirements to accommodate them.

All NHS chiropodists must be state registered, which means they have passed the examination of the Society of Chiropodists, for which the minimum educational qualifications are five GCSE passes (A–C) with two A levels including English and at least one science subject.

The three-year, full-time course which leads to the examination is offered by 12 recognised schools in the country. The first year entails an introductory life skills course which combines theoretical and practical work. The second year includes anatomy and physiology with obvious regard to the foot. The written and oral examinations cover chiropody, physiology, and anatomy, and a practical examination. In the third year students study the principles of medicine and surgery with application to foot disorders, eptiology, pathology, diagnosis of foot abnormalities together with the theory and practice of therapeutics.

Students are also required to take written and oral examinations and two sessions of practical chiropody. Successful completion of the course enables candidates to apply for state registration.

Other jobs
Occupational Therapist; Nurse; Physiotherapist; Physiotherapy Helper; Chiropractor

Contact
Society of Chiropodists, 53 Welbeck Street, London W1M 7HE; 071-486 3381

Institute of Chiropodists, 91 Lord Street, Southport, Merseyside PR8 1SA; 0704 46141

Classroom Assistant (Non Teaching)

Hours	These will depend on the requirements of the school, but it is usual for part-time classroom assistants to cover either five morning or five afternoon sessions
Pay	£3.83–£4.47 per hour
Personal qualities	Practical; attentive; good with children; imaginative

For a mother seeking a part-time job which will fit around her other domestic responsibilities, working in a school may be the perfect answer.

Many non-teaching appointments such as secretaries, lunch-time supervisors, clerks, or classroom assistants (sometimes referred to as nannies or helpers) are in such great demand that in many cases the applicants far outweigh the vacancies.

The classroom assistant is generally a back-up for the form teacher whose sole job is to teach.

In the majority of mainstream schools the classroom assistant can take some of the workload from the teacher, listening to the younger children reading, or helping with other projects in the class, such as painting, cutting out, making models, singing etc, and when another adult is required on class outings it is usual for the classroom assistant to accompany them. A classroom assistant normally works alongside another auxiliary, often a teenager on Youth Training.

For someone who enjoys being in the company of children, can show limitless patience and understanding, yet still retain an air of authority, being a classroom assistant can be rewarding.

Qualifications and experience
Qualifications depend very much on the individual school's

requirements. A National Nursery Examination Board Certificate (NNEB) is useful. It takes two years to get the certificate
and some colleges expect applicants to have several GCSE
passes (A–C) before giving them a place on the course. The
course incorporates academic study and work experience in
certain placements such as schools, hospitals or nurseries.

For further information about the Certificate write to:
National Nursery Examination Board, 8 Chequer Street, St
Albans, Hertfordshire AL1 3XZ; 0727 867333. The Board also
has offices in Wales and Northern Ireland and the Scottish
equivalent is: The Scottish Nursery Nurses Board, 6 Kilnford
Crescent, Dundonald, Kilmarnock KAT 90W; 0563 850057.

Other jobs
Auxiliary Assistant; Midday Supervisor; Escort; Clerk in a
school; School Crossing Patrol

Contact
Local education authority

Cleaner

Hours	Depend on the employer who may require an hour or two a day, five or six days per week. Some school cleaners may be required to work only part of the school holidays
Pay	Usually not less than £3 per hour but varies from region to region
Personal qualities	Honest; discreet; pleasant; dependable; conscientious

Opportunities for cleaners are many and varied. Vacancies
occur in every walk of life: the busy hospital, the doctor's
surgery, the local pub, the library, local council offices, shops

and private homes – this must surely be one job where the vacancies far outweigh the applicants.

Cleaners often have to work as part of a team as many companies employ women to clean in a large office complex, factory or department store. Cleaners may be called in to work several hours when the building has closed in the evenings or in the early morning before business or school commences.

There are also opportunities to clean private houses which can be combined with household duties (see Home Help).

Qualifications and experience
No formal qualifications are required to be a cleaner, but experience in the cleaning business may be an advantage.

Many cleaners who decide to go it alone have been employed for a number of years and therefore know the ins and outs, the best kinds of material to use, the quickest way to clean a floor etc.

Other jobs
Shelf Filler; Petrol Pump Attendant; Counter Assistant; Kitchen Assistant

Contacts
Ads in shop windows; friends and neighbours

Clerk

Hours	Approximately 20 hours per week
Pay	£2.60–£3 per hour
Personal qualities	Neat; clear handwriting; methodical; accurate; numerate; able to work alone or as member of team

A general clerk performs a variety of duties in an office, such as issuing and checking forms, recording information and updating information, maintaining accurate records, filing, preparing statements, ordering merchandise and checking stock levels, dealing with queries and complaints from customers over the telephone, transmitting telex and fax messages and possibly sorting and distributing incoming mail.

Depending on the size of the organisation a general clerk may be responsible for doing all or some of the duties described above.

Clerks in large firms can probably train to become section leaders or supervisors.

Qualifications and experience

Employers expect staff to have had a good standard of education and also to possess some GCSE passes (A–C); the most important subjects are English and maths but others regarded as useful are: accounts, typing and office practice. Many firms recruit applicants with a BTEC Certificate or Royal Society of Arts (RSA) qualifications while other employers allow their staff to study by attending day-release courses, although this is unlikely to apply to part-timers.

Training for clerical work often takes place on the job under the supervision of an experienced member of staff. Some firms run short instruction classes.

No formal qualifications are required for the BTEC General Certificate/Diploma courses. The Certificate involves one year of part-time study, while the Diploma course is two years part time.

Students must have four GCSE passes (A–C) or hold a BTEC General award in order to study for the BTEC National Certificate/Diploma. It is two years' part-time study for the Certificate course and a two-year part-time/three-year sandwich course for the Diploma.

Students with one A level and three GCSE passes (A–C) or a BTEC National award are able to study for the BTEC Higher National Certificate/Diploma. The Certificate is a two-year, part-time course and the Diploma a two-year part-time or three-year sandwich course. Students who aspire to supervisory or management posts will find these awards very useful.

The Royal Society of Arts (RSA), the London Chamber of

Commerce and Industry and Pitman Examinations Institute all offer qualifications in typing, word processing, shorthand, shorthand-typing and audio-typing, clerical work, office practice and secretarial duties. These courses generally last one year full-time or two years part-time.

Other jobs
Accounts Clerk

Contact
Write to: Pitman Examinations Institute, Catteshall Manor, Catteshall Lane, Godalming, Surrey GU7 1UU; 04868 5311

Cold Canvassing

Hours	Approximately 20 hours per week
Pay	£3.50 per hour plus expenses
Personal qualities	Smart; pleasant; persuasive; fit and strong; good at communicating; enjoys working outdoors; able to drive an advantage

Many companies employ canvassers to go out among the public to introduce and promote their products.

One method is for canvassers to call on homes and tell householders about the product. This personal approach is often preferred as it gives the potential customers the ideal opportunity to ask questions about the goods. Such canvassers are usually car owners, and able to transport catalogues, goods or samples, and if a prospective customer shows an interest, then follow it up.

The alternative is for canvassers to converge on the high streets and approach shoppers and passers-by.

In both cases training is given.

Qualifications and experience
Personal attributes are more important than formal qualifications but all staff are expected to have a good standard of general education. Someone who has had experience of retail selling or interviewing would be well placed to take up such employment.

Other jobs
Interviewing; Retail Selling; Merchandising

Contact
Write to mail order and other companies employing direct marketing techniques, eg double glazing firms.

Cook

Hours	May work 9 or 10am to 2pm; it really does depend on the employer
Pay	In licensed hotels not less than £2.12 per hour; in unlicensed hotels not less than £2.38 per hour
Personal qualities	Flair and aptitude for cooking; fit; healthy; able to work under pressure

A cook is usually employed to prepare a large number of meals for people. Areas in which there is most part-time employment for women may be in schools, hospitals, or company canteens. Cooks often work alongside other kitchen staff who deal with the preparation of the food, including cleaning vegetables, peeling and cutting fruit, filleting fish.

A cook must be fully conversant with the various cooking techniques, know the best ways of preserving food and of cooking it. She must have a knowledge of special diets and be able to prepare food to look both appetising and attractive.

It is the cook's responsibility to make sure food is stored

hygienically; there is paperwork to attend to and utensils to check and put away. Kitchen hygiene is another area for which the cook is largely responsible.

Cake making and decoration is a branch of cooking often carried out by individuals in their own homes. A reputable cake maker commands high prices.

Qualifications and experience
It is quite possible for mature applicants to train as cooks by undertaking a full-time training course. There are no formal qualifications required for entry on to most of these courses although a good general education is important and some City & Guilds courses ask for three GCSE passes, one of which should include English.

One of the more popular ways to train is with an employer, studying for the City & Guilds qualification on a day- or block-release basis, which usually takes a year. Students should first check with employers to find out if they allow time off to study for the C&G Certificate.

The National Health Service also runs a trainee cook scheme (C&G 706) at certain hospitals which involves day release over two years.

Other jobs
Bar Staff; Kitchen Assistant; Counter Service Assistant

Contact
Job Centre for further information on NHS Schemes

Counter Service Assistant

Hours	Often required to work unsocial hours. High demand for part-timers during the tourist season

Pay	Not less than £2.38 per hour
Personal qualities	Able to get on with people; healthy; good with cash; clean; smart; polite; tactful

Counter service assistants are employed in self-service restaurants, cafes, snack bars, or in whatever catering establishment customers are required to serve themselves.

Her duties include: cleaning the crockery, cutlery and trays in readiness for the customers; undertaking basic tasks, for example, washing salad, preparing simple dishes, making sandwiches, cutting up meat and vegetables, opening tins; filling coffee machines, serving meals, snacks and drinks from behind the counter. She may also price the meal and take money from customers.

She is also responsible for keeping the counter area clean and cleaning up food spillages, wiping down tables, gathering up dirty dishes, emptying ash trays, refilling sauce bottles, sweeping floors and any other domestic duties.

Training is done on the job under the supervision of an experienced member of staff. Many large organisations have formal training programmes where new recruits receive a short period of off-the-job training, which might include an induction course to familiarise them with the company and its policies, conditions of employment and other such matters. Instruction might also include health and safety, and the more practical aspects of using the cash register, changing the till roll, presenting food etc.

Qualifications and experience
Most employers expect their staff to have a good standard of general education and some GCSE passes (A-C).

There are also opportunities for assistants to take the City & Guilds 700/4 Counter Service Assistant's Specific Skills Certificate. These schemes normally last for six to eight weeks and cover: counter service skills, tools and equipment, working practices and procedures etc. Training is mainly supplemented by a few hours each week of formal off-the-job instruction. Each trainee has to complete a course work assessment, a knowledge and practical skills test. Successful candidates are awarded a certificate.

Other jobs
Kitchen Assistant; Waitress; Checkout Operator; Midday Supervisor; Bar Staff

Contact
Write to: Hotel and Catering Training Company, International House, High Street, Ealing, London W5 5DB; 081-579 2400

Court Reporter

Hours	Most work freelance – often irregular and very long hours
Pay	Remuneration reflects the number of hours worked. A newly qualified court reporter earns around £10,000 full time
Personal qualities	Accurate; discreet; honest; trustworthy; good hearing

Court reporters, often known as shorthand writers, attend court sittings and write down the complete report of the evidence, the judgment and sometimes the speeches of counsel. While most still use shorthand, computer-aided transcription is being introduced.

A court reporter must be able to work at high speed and is responsible for summarising and typing up an account of the proceedings afterwards, if required. Occasionally she may have to check legal details in libraries.

Although an extremely interesting job, it can also be very lonely, and court reporters feel under enormous pressure because they are totally responsible for taking down all the necessary information. A reporter can also find employment at public enquiries, business conferences and board meetings, and there are opportunities to work abroad.

Qualifications and experience

Employers expect applicants to have some GCSE passes (A-C) and some require A-levels. Applicants need proven ability in shorthand or stenotyping (usually over 150 words per minute), good typing speeds and a thorough knowledge of grammar and punctuation.

There are many full and part-time courses available, including evening classes which include various shorthand languages. The entry requirements for these courses vary, although most colleges expect a minimum of four GCSE passes (A-C) including English language. Those applying to private schools may find the requirements less demanding.

Those firms in London and the provinces who have appointments from the Lord Chancellor to register court proceedings undertake the training of court reporters. Length of training depends on the qualifications and experience of the individual. Candidates who already possess good shorthand or stenotyping speeds and the relevant experience in law or business could become fully qualified in three months, but 12 months is more usual. Throughout this period trainees work alongside experienced court reporters, increasing shorthand or stenotyping speeds and familiarising themselves with court jargon and procedures.

A trainee court reporter is not allowed to sit alone until she has passed a practical examination in court. At this stage she is known as a provisionally accredited court reporter. Fully trained and with a minimum of three years' experience of working without supervision, she must take a written and practical examination before being admitted to a roll of accredited court reporters.

Court reporters may join the Institute of Shorthand Writers, initially as an associate and after passing the relevant examinations, become a member.

The Institute of Shorthand Writers and the Association of Professional Shorthand Writers are both able to supply a list of member firms who train and employ court reporters.

Other jobs

Freelance Journalism; Interviewing; Secretary

Contact

Write to: The Institute of Shorthand Writers, 2 New Square, Lincoln's Inn, London WC2A 3RU; 071-405 9884

The Secretary, The Association of Professional Shorthand Writers, 6 Jellyman Close, Blake Brook, Kidderminster DY11 6AD

Cutter

Hours	Variable
Pay	Usually paid according to skill, often paid piecework
Personal qualities	Reliable; adaptable; good eyesight; steady hand; interested in fashion; numerate; able to follow instructions

A cutter is employed in the clothing industry. The job involves far more than cutting out material for making up into garments. Cutters may be employed in large textile companies and responsible for cutting out bundles of material or they may work in close association with a bespoke tailor.

Some outfitters might employ fully experienced cutters who wish to work from home.

Before laying out the pattern on the chosen fabric, they must first check that the material is devoid of flaws or unsightly marks. Once the patterns have been arranged, allowing for any shrinkage that may occur, their position is clearly marked on the cloth in readiness for cutting out. The most common method is to use shears or an electric knife where greater precision is needed. In large factories where many layers of cloth are being cut, a mechanised process called die cutting is employed. After the cloth has been cut it is numbered and made up into bundles for the next stage of production.

Qualifications and experience
For those without recognised qualifications the only way to gain entry is by completing a course which can take up to five years. No formal qualifications are required for entry on to such a course but some GCSEs are an obvious advantage (maths, English and art).

Trainees are taught about the various types of fabric and all the possible defects, how to decipher written and oral instructions, how to cut out etc. Those who have had experience, perhaps as a dressmaker, or those who have taken a recognised course will find it much easier to secure employment as a cutter.

Other jobs
Alteration Hand; Sewing Machinist; Tailor/Dressmaker; Garment Examiner

Contact
Job Centre (enquire about training schemes)

Write to: CAPITB plc, 80 Richardshaw Lane, Pudsey, Leeds LS28 6BN; 0532 393355 for further information on courses and colleges

Dental Surgery Assistant/Receptionist

Hours	Depends on the dental practice
Pay	Relates to the payment structure regulated by the local Area Health Authority
Personal qualities	Clean and tidy; fit; calm; friendly; good at dealing with people; untroubled by the sight of blood

A dental surgery assistant offers support and back-up to the dentist. Her duties include greeting patients when they arrive, marking up the patient's record card, ensuring that the surgery is kept clean and tidy and processing X-rays. When the dentist is treating a patient the dental assistant is on hand to pass over instruments, mix filling composites and impression materials, and keep the patient's mouth clean during operations. In some practices the dental assistant combines her role with reception and clerical duties: keeping the records up to date, making appointments, receiving payment for work carried out, checking on stock levels and answering the telephone.

Obviously roles differ between practices. Part-time work may be available in general practice and possibly dental hospitals although this will depend on the Area Health Authority.

Qualifications and experience

Because there is no age limit the dentist decides whether an applicant is the right person to undertake training as a dental surgery assistant.

To study for the National Certificate of the Examining Board for Dental Surgery Assistants (RDSA) students should have two GCSE passes (A–C), preferably including English and biology.

Much of the training is done on the job and in many cases is supplemented by attending an RDSA National Certificate course on a day-release basis or evening classes. Wolsey Hall College in Oxford runs a correspondence course leading to an oral exam, written paper and practical tests.

For those training with a hospital there is a hospital certificate of proficiency course recognised by the Association of Dental Hospitals. The certificate has two stages: Intermediate and Final. Those applicants aged over 18 who have two GCSE passes (A–C) or their equivalent can sit for the National Certificate once they have finished a two-year chairside experience.

During training students cover anatomy and physiology; nursing principles as applied to dentistry and the care of patients; methods of sterilisation; preparation of filling and impression materials etc.

Other jobs
Receptionist; Nursing Auxiliary; Secretary

Contact
Information on job opportunities for dental surgery assistants may be obtained by writing to: The Secretary, The Association of British Dental Surgery Assistants, DSA House, 29 London Street, Fleetwood, Lancashire FY7 6JY; 03917 78631

Dentist

Hours	Several days per week depending on the practice
Pay	The average salary for dentists employed full time in general practice is £26,915. Dentists employed in hospitals are paid according to hospital grades
Personal qualities	Sympathetic; patient; good eyesight; dexterous; reassuring manner; able to work as a member of team

Dentists may be employed in general practice, hospital work, community dentistry, and for those highly qualified, teaching posts exist in dental schools or universities.

The duties of a dentist in general practice include diagnosing and treating diseases of the mouth and teeth. In her daily work she examines patients' teeth, takes X-rays, gives injections, drills and fills cavities, extracts teeth, fits dental appliances such as braces or dentures and occasionally prescribes drugs. Nowadays dental care is far more concerned with preventive treatment, and a dentist is able to offer advice on caring for teeth.

Qualifications and experience

To qualify, a dentist must have a degree in dental surgery or a diploma as a Licentiate in Dental Surgery, and be registered in the Dentists' Register which is maintained by the General Dental Council. It takes five or six years to study for a degree in Dental Surgery at one of the 16 dental schools in the UK and competition for places is stiff. Entry requirements are A levels in physics, chemistry and biology but some schools run pre-dental courses for students who have not attained the appropriate subjects or satisfactory grades. For further information about courses contact the General Dental Council.

Students who are exempt from the pre-dental course go straight into the pre-clinical year which involves the study of oral anatomy, general anatomy, histology, biochemistry and physiology.

During the final stage, which lasts four years, students deal with patients and learn practical dental skills. Training is undertaken in general and dental hospitals and out-patient clinics. All aspects of dentistry are covered including: dental prosthetics, using various dental materials, children's dentistry, operating techniques, preventive dentistry, orthodontics (methods of correcting irregularities in the teeth and jaw), oral surgery, community dentistry, together with periodontology, radiology, oral pathology, oral medicine and pharmacology. In the third and fourth years students treat patients under supervision.

It would take a high level of commitment for someone to undertake this arduous training for the purpose of part-time work only, but it is not uncommon for mature students to go into dentistry, especially if they already have a degree in a related subject.

Other jobs

Dental Surgery Assistant; Laboratory Technician; Nurse

Contact

Dental schools

Specialist publications in which vacancies appear: *British Dental Journal*

Write to: The General Dental Council, 37 Wimpole Street, London W1M 8DQ; 071-486 2171

The British Dental Association, 64 Wimpole Street, London W1M 8AL; 071-935 0875

Dietitian

Hours	Several days per week
Pay	Full-time NHS salaries start from £9640 for basic grades rising to £22,495
Personal qualities	Tolerant; persuasive; interested in people; good communicator; scientifically minded; practical; able to understand people's problems and to relate to them

A dietitian offers advice and devises special diets for people who require them, ie people with diabetes; the elderly; parents with large families; people suffering from a medical condition which warrants their following a special diet, and anyone else who is referred to them. There are many areas in which dietitians may be employed. The largest employers are hospitals in which they work closely with the medical staff.

They may also find employment in out-patient clinics to which people are referred by their GPs; research provides other opportunities for dietitians to work alongside biochemists, statisticians and physicists. In these circumstances they may be asked to measure various diets and evaluate a patient's consumption of nutrients.

Although the NHS is the largest employer vacancies also occur in: large catering organisations, government departments, the education service, medical research and industry; they may also work in the community dealing with members of the general public, giving talks and demonstrations to weight control groups, schools and colleges.

Many dietitians diversify and concentrate more on the

media: writing articles, giving radio talks, and appearing on television.

Qualifications and experience

Mature applicants with the relevant experience are accepted by many colleges and it is the kind of occupation one may re-enter after a career break.

To practise in the NHS dietitians must be registered by the Dietitians' Board of the Council for Professions Supplementary to Medicine.

To gain entry into the profession a degree is required for which the entry qualifications are: two A levels (chemistry and another science) and three GCSE passes (A–C) usually including two sciences and English.

Applicants holding an approved degree or postgraduate diploma are able to register.

Other jobs

Laboratory Technician

Contact

Regular lists of vacancies are published by the British Dietetic Association. See the CRAC *Directory of Further Education* for lists of colleges which run courses in dietetics.

Write to: The British Dietetic Association, 7th Floor, Elizabeth House, 22 Suffolk Street, Queensway, Birmingham B1 1LS; 021-643 5483 (please send SAE)

Dish Washer

Hours	May work on a casual basis
Pay	Approximately £2.60 per hour
Personal qualities	Clean; reliable; stamina

A dish washer may be employed in a hotel, restaurant, pub, school, hospital, or any other place where food is prepared and served.

Her duties involve clearing away and washing up the continual influx of dirty dishes, stacking them away and perhaps lending a hand with the other general duties in the kitchen when, and if, time allows.

Occasionally opportunities arise to work on a casual basis when large functions are organised or when, say, the local civic centre holds a banquet and needs to employ more domestic staff to cover it.

Qualifications and experience
No qualifications are required to be a dishwasher. It is not a particularly easy job standing for hours washing an endless stream of dirty dishes, in a sometimes hot and sticky atmosphere. It is not really suitable for women who have skin problems.

Other jobs
Kitchen Assistant; Midday Supervisor; Cook; Tea Lady

Contact
Postcards in windows

Dispensing Optician

Hours	Several days per week
Pay	After registration opticians employed full time can earn £12,000
Personal qualities	Patient; accurate; numerate; dexterous; able to get on with people

A dispensing optician translates the prescriptions which are supplied by the ophthalmic surgeon or ophthalmic optician, using complex apparatus to measure, fit and supply spectacles, contact lenses and artificial eyes. She discusses with the patient the type of frame that is most suitable in terms of size and colour, and ensures that it fits perfectly. Her job could also include supplying apparatus to opticians and laboratories, and sunglasses, binoculars etc to the general public.

Vacancies occur within private practice, hospitals, and a small number of dispensing opticians work for firms as consultants. There are a few teaching posts available in colleges and universities too.

Qualifications and experience

Provided mature applicants have had ten years' experience in optical work, the entry requirements for training courses are waived. However, if their maths is not up to GCSE, they may have difficulty keeping up with the work.

Training normally lasts three years. Candidates undertake a full-time, two-year course at a college plus one year practical experience, or combine three years' practical experience with a part-time day release/correspondence course. Entry requirements: five GCSE passes (A–C) which should include a science subject, English and maths. Both methods lead to the qualifying examinations of the Fellowship of the Association of British Dispensing Opticians. Success entitles the dispensing optician to register with the General Optical Council which in turn will enable her to practise in the UK.

Other jobs
Orthoptist

Contact
Specialist publications include *The Optician*

Write to: The Association of British Dispensing Opticians, 6 Hurlingham Business Park, Sullivan Road, London SW6 3DM; 071-935 7411

General Optical Council, 41 Harley Street, London W1N 1DJ; 071-580 3898

Distributor

Hours	From two to thirty hours per week. Will vary according to the job
Pay	May be paid on an hourly basis or on the quantity of material delivered: £8-£16 per 1000
Personal qualities	Physically fit; honest; flexible; enjoy working outdoors

Many companies use the services of a distributor when they are sending out leaflets or complimentary samples of a recently launched product. Distributors are normally assigned to cover certain areas and to complete their deliveries within a set time.

As a rule there is no formal training, but advice on how to get out as many leaflets in as short a time as possible is usually offered by other distributors who have learnt the tricks of the trade.

Qualifications and experience
No qualifications are required for this job but obviously experience counts for a great deal as you will find you are able to deliver more quickly if you have established a routine.

Other jobs
Party Plan; Mail Order Agent; School Crossing Patrol

District and Community Nurse

Hours	Shift work
Pay	Depends on experience and qualifications but will include expenses. Full-time salaries £13,740–£15,900 when acting as midwife and health visitor
Personal qualities	Good listener; tactful; tolerant; able to work independently and to take responsibility; physically strong; not easily upset; unflappable; able to drive

Nursing is one of the professions which welcomes the return of staff on a part-time basis and accepts mature trainees.

A District Enrolled Nurse (DEN) is responsible for providing skilled nursing care for patients in their own homes or in residential care establishments. Her practical nursing duties include: administering injections, applying dressings, draining wounds, removing stitches, washing and cleaning her patients, and offering support and encouragement at all times.

Once a patient is released from hospital a district nurse usually visits at least once a day, to give medication and any other treatment as required. District nurses work closely with social workers, occupational therapists and voluntary agencies as well as hospital colleagues and other members of the health team. In some rural areas, a district nurse may take on the responsibilities of health visitor and midwife whenever the situation arises.

Because of recent changes in the aftercare of psychiatric patients, many district and community nurses provide health care and advice to those who are discharged into the community after hospitalisation.

Qualifications and experience

To become a district and community nurse it is necessary to qualify as a general nurse first.

To qualify for the National Certificate in District Nursing (NDN Cert) applicants should have a minimum of five GCSE passes (A–C), or satisfy the college selection standards. She must also be qualified as a Registered General Nurse (RGN) (Part 1 of the Register) and also possess nursing experience. Some colleges require their staff to sit an entrance test.

Provided that fully qualified and experienced Enrolled Nurses (EN) meet the requirements of the individual school or college, they are able to train for the DEN Certificate. In most circumstances a driving licence is necessary.

The NDN Certificate course is a nine months' full-time course and includes a period of supervised clinical practice. These courses take place at colleges of further and higher education, polytechnics and universities with subjects including psychology, physiology, sociology and epidemiology. Written and oral communication skills are also taught.

The DEN Certificate course is a 16-week, full-time course, usually based in the same college and following the same format, although perhaps not as intensely, as the NDN Certificate.

Other jobs

General Nurse; Nursing Auxiliary; Voluntary Nursing

Contact

Regional Nursing Officer at any of the NHS Regional Health Authorities.

Dog Beautician

Hours   Flexible

Pay   No national standard. Most dog beauticians are self-employed

Personal qualities   Able to handle dogs; tolerant; pleasant; confident; eye for detail; accurate

A dog beautician (more commonly known as dog trimmer, or canine beautician) ensures that the dogs are kept in tip-top condition by regular grooming and trimming. Other duties may involve washing and drying the animals, brushing coats, clipping nails, cleaning teeth and ears (treating for parasites whenever necessary). She may prepare dogs for shows.

Qualifications and experience
The mature recruit can become a dog beautician. The two main methods of training are by becoming an apprentice with an employer or attending a fee-paying course, although the former may prove to be somewhat more difficult for the mature applicant.

No formal qualifications are required for entry on to a training programme. The fee-paying courses are particularly relevant to older students and are available at many privately run training establishments. Courses may last from one or two weeks to one year but this depends on what is covered by the syllabus.

The City & Guilds 775 Certificate in Dog Grooming is an award given to those candidates who have successfully undertaken a series of skills tests organised by the Pet Trade and Industry Association. Applicants are able to sit for the skills test whether or not they have had any formal training. The tests, which take place at appointed centres, involve the applicants in preparing the dogs: trimming, bathing, grooming etc, using both hand and power tools.

Having gained the basic knowledge of dog grooming, it may be useful to do some voluntary cleaning up chores in a dog parlour before embarking on one's own career. Or contact a dog beautician and ask if it is possible to work alongside her for a while to watch her techniques.

Anyone who suffers from skin complaints or who may be allergic to animals should avoid this work.

Other jobs
Animal Minder; Veterinary Nurse; Dog Walker

Contact
Pet Trade and Industry Association, 103 High Street, Bedford
MK40 1NE; 0234 273933

Dog Walker

Hours	An hour or two per day
Pay	£1 per hour
Personal qualities	Fresh air enthusiast; reliable; trustworthy; animal lover; physically fit; caring

Jobs working with animals, such as an RSPCA officer, animal technician, kennel worker, are usually full time. However, there are other ways in which a love of animals can be combined with a part-time job, and one is by becoming a dog walker.

Anybody who owns a dog and is working full time needs to ensure that their dog is exercised each day. When a dog walker is employed, the owner needs to trust this stranger, be sure she has a genuine love and understanding of dogs and will take the animal out each day, and not merely allow it to run in the garden for a short spell.

Dog walking won't make anyone a millionaire but it is healthy and a worthwhile service.

Qualifications and experience
No formal qualifications are required.

Before taking on such a responsibility, both dog and minder should meet several times so that they are not total strangers.

Other jobs
Dog Beautician; Veterinary Nurse

Contact
Advertise your service in pet shop windows; inform vets of your service; place an advertisement in the local newspaper

Driving Instructor

Hours	Hours will be dictated by the number of pupils
Pay	Full-time instructors can earn £134–£200 per week depending on the area and the number of pupils
Personal qualities	Patient; tactful; unflappable; alert; able to put people at ease; mechanically minded

A driving instructor is responsible for teaching people to drive properly in preparation for the driving test.

Many people claim that they are able to teach someone else to drive, but doing it correctly is another matter. Many instructors begin their careers working for others, and later branch off into self-employment. There will always be a need for good, well qualified instructors.

Qualifications and experience
Mature applicants are often preferred.

In order to become an Approved Driving Instructor, the applicant must have been in possession of a driving licence for four out of the last six years, not have had any disqualification within that time, be fit and healthy and also pass a qualifying examination.

It is an offence for anyone who is not qualified as an Approved Driving Instructor to teach professionally. It is unusual for anyone aged under 23 to gain Approved Driving Instructor (ADI) registration.

Before an instructor is allowed to teach anyone to drive she must first pass the Department of Transport's examinations.

There is a two-hour written paper in which various aspects of driving are covered, successful completion of which leads to the two-hour practical examination in which the driver's own skills are put under scrutiny with the instructor taking the role of the pupil.

Most trainees study at home for the examination and undertake professional training at a reputable driving school. This generally lasts one to three weeks. While some schools concentrate on just one area, others offer both theoretical and practical training. As the syllabus and standard of instruction differ from school to school, it is wise to check them out carefully.

Experienced driving instructors wishing to become tutors attend a four-week course in which skills are developed. These high-level driving tests are run by the Department of Transport Examiners Training Establishments.

Those seeking to work with established driving schools need to apply for a trainee licence. This is a provisional licence issued by the ADI Registrar, which is valid for only six months, enabling candidates to gain practical experience before sitting the examinations. After qualifying, the applicant's name is put on to the ADI register, and an official certificate issued. It must be renewed every four years, at which time instructors may be required to undergo a test of ability and fitness in order to continue to instruct.

The Associated Examining Board with the Driving Instructors' Association have together developed a professional qualification for ADIs, the Diploma in Driving Instruction. Courses are available through local further education colleges and study material from the Driving Instructors' Association.

Other jobs
Driving Tutor, Cab Driver

Contact
Write to: Register of Approved Driving Instructors, Department of Transport, Room C193, 2 Marsham Street, London SW1P 3EB

Details of National Joint Council tutors: John Milne, 121

Marshalswick Lane, St Albans, Hertfordshire AL1 4UX; 0727 58068

National Association of Approved Driving Instructors, 90 Ash Lane, Hale Barns, Altrincham, Cheshire WA15 8PB; 061-980 5907

Dry Cleaning Operator

Hours	Approximately 26 hours per week but obviously this will vary between employers
Pay	Depends on training, experience and employer. Not less than £1.80 per hour
Personal qualities	Pleasant; neat; quick; helpful; methodical

Those employed in a dry cleaning shop may find their time divided between working on the counter and working behind the scenes. Some establishments carry out garment cleaning on the premises, others have a main operational plant to which all the garments are transported for dry cleaning.

The dry cleaning operator checks garments brought into the shop, and then hands a receipt to the customer before fixing an identifying ticket on to the garment. All garments are sorted and those which are heavily stained must be put to one side and dealt with separately. The garments are then cleaned and pressed. Finally, the garments are checked before being covered with large polythene bags, ready for collection by the customers.

When working on the counter the assistant may deal with cash and handle customers' queries.

Qualifications and experience
Most employers prefer applicants to have had a good standard of general education. Training is carried out under the supervision of fully experienced staff.

Interested workers who are thought to be suitable may be

encouraged to attend further training courses, thereby increasing both their knowledge and practical skills. These courses were initiated by the Fabric Care Research Association who together with the Textile Services Association Cleaning and Rental Services Ltd form the Textile Care and Rental Industry Council for Education. The courses last from one to four days and normally take place at the FCRA Laboratories in Harrogate, Yorkshire. Subjects include stain removal techniques, introduction to textiles and laundry bleaching and how to deal with fabrics such as leather and silk.

There are some evening classes in London which together with some of the short day classes lead to examinations of the Guild of Cleaners and Launderers (GCL), the certificates of which are widely recognised.

Other jobs
Garment Examiner; Retail Assistant; Hotel Room Attendant; Laundry Work

Contact
Write to: The Fabric Care Research Association, Forest House Laboratories, Knaresborough Road, Harrogate, North Yorkshire HG2 7LZ; 0423 885977

The Textile Services Association, 7 Churchill Court, 58 Station Road, North Harrow, Middlesex HA2 7SA; 081-863 7755/8658

Florist

Hours	Possibility of work at weekends and during busy periods for weddings etc. Could also be self-employed
Pay	No national scale, so rates are very much up

to the employer. Full-time qualified florists
can earn £65–£200 per week

Personal qualities   Artistic; creative; dexterous; patient;
pleasant; eye for colour and shape;
physically fit; able to follow instructions

A florist is responsible for making plants and flowers into
various arrangements as ordered by the customer, including
wreaths, posies, wedding bouquets or sprays. Depending on
the size of the shop, her other duties could include checking
and delivering orders, buying flowers from the market, and
selling them in the shop.

Some florists travel around visiting hotels or large firms to
arrange displays for special occasions.

Self-employment opportunities exist for gifted amateur
gardeners and also flower arrangers who have an extensive
knowledge of flowers and arrangement techniques.

Qualifications and experience
Employers expect staff to have a good standard of general
education and it would be useful to hold GCSE passes (A–C)
in English, maths, biology, and an art subject.

The usual entry into floristry is through getting a job in a
florist's shop and studying part time at a college of further
education. The Society of Floristry has a list of all the colleges
which run courses.

The trainee florist is taught how to take care of flowers and
plants, learns their correct names, is shown how to wire and
mount flowers, and how to gift wrap flowers.

The courses which are available include: (a) The City &
Guilds Floristry 019 is usually undertaken on block/day-
release basis. The C&G course is, at the moment, under review
and a fourth stage in Business Procedures directed toward
supervisors and managers in floristry is being piloted at a
number of centres. (b) A full-time BTEC National Diploma in
Floristry and Flower Production is currently operating at the
Welsh College of Horticulture. Entrants are required to have
four GCSE passes (A–C). A two-year sandwich course is also
available.

There are also many privately run courses.

The Society of Floristry ensures that constant high examination standards are maintained throughout the industry. They also offer examinations themselves.

Other jobs
Window Dresser; Retail Assistant

Contact
Write to: The Society of Floristry Ltd, The Secretary, Old School House, Payford, Redmarley, Gloucestershire GL19 3HY; 05231 820809 (enclose SAE)

British Retail Florists Association, 24 Market Place, Sleaford, Lincolnshire NG34 7AS; 0529 413712 (enclose SAE)

For a syllabus of courses and colleges: City & Guilds of London Institute (address on page 151)

Garment Examiner

Hours	Shift work
Pay	Wages Council minimum rate is £1.98 per hour
Personal qualities	Patient; good eyesight; quick; experienced in sewing; meticulous

As garments pass through each stage of production they are inspected for faults. The final inspection, before the garment is despatched, is carried out by the garment examiner.

A garment examiner must be thorough and work with written documentation relating to each garment detailing its measurements etc. A note must be made of any faults on a report sheet. Each garment carries an identification label indicating who was responsible for each stage in its manufacture. If any faults are found the garment is returned to the person responsible who must then rectify the problem.

Qualifications and experience
No formal qualifications are required to be a garment examiner. Many are already experienced sewing machinists and so know what to look out for.

Some companies give aptitude and eyesight tests to applicants. It is customary for employers to arrange their own training schemes.

Other jobs
Sewing Machinist; Tailoress/Dressmaker; Window Dresser; Quality Control Inspector

Groundswoman

Hours	May vary: weekend, seasonal, or casual
Pay	Present full-time salaries range between £4.30 per hour for a head groundsman/woman and £2.70 per hour for an unskilled assistant
Personal qualities	Able to undertake manual jobs; fit; reliable; able to drive an advantage

The job of a groundswoman includes the overall maintenance of outdoor playing areas, covering all kinds of recreational sport including rugby, football, tennis, golf etc.

Not only must she ensure that pitches and greens are kept in first class condition by mowing, re-seeding, turfing, weeding and watering, but also be responsible for tending any herbaceous flowerbeds. She may be called upon to dig drainage ditches when required and also to offer assistance when sporting events are taking place. Other responsibilities include the regular maintenance of equipment and occasionally to drive vehicles on the highways.

The main employers for groundsmen/women are local authorities, sports clubs and contracting firms.

Qualifications and experience
Places on training programmes are difficult to get, which is why GCSE passes (A–C) in biology, maths and chemistry would increase your chances. Some employers set a medical examination.

Promotion to head groundswoman is primarily based on a combination of experience and ability; however, the examinations of the Institute of Groundsmanship are gaining wide acceptance:

The National Practical/Technical Certificates in Sportsground Maintenance are intended for working ground staff and available by day release and evening class.

The Intermediate Diploma Certificate is available to all those who have a National Technical Certificate but on a limited basis by both evening class and day release.

The National Diploma in Science and Practice of Turfculture and Sportsground Management is a higher qualification for those going into management.

Scheme A – for those employed by the local authority – offers opportunities for entry into other types of employment such as cultivating shrubs and trees. There are other courses available which include on-the-job training and block release at college, covering ornamental gardening, groundsmanship, nursery work, and agriculture.

Scheme B – the Phase 1 City & Guilds Certificate in Horticulture and the Phase 2 Certificate in Amenity Horticulture – is a higher qualification for local authority workers which is also available in some private sectors.

The sporting enthusiast who would welcome the outdoor life combined with her favourite sporting pastime is likely to enjoy such a job.

Other jobs
Gardener

Contact
Write to local sports clubs

Write to the Institute of Groundsmanship, 19–23 Church Street, The Agora, Wolverton, Milton Keynes, Buckinghamshire MK12 5LG; 0908 312511

Hairdresser

Hours	Variable
Pay	This depends very much on experience. The minimum hourly rate is £2.40. Hairdressers usually increase their income from customers' tips
Personal qualities	Able to get on with people; good eyesight; physically fit; smart; patient; clean; creative; caring

Hairdressers not only wash and cut hair but also set, perm, colour, bleach, and blow dry; answer questions about hair-dressing preparations and hairstyles, so an up-to-date knowledge is important.

They may offer counselling on problems associated with the scalp, and in a men's salon (although many accommodate both sexes these days) a man may require his moustache or beard to be trimmed.

Hairdressers may be employed in hospitals, department stores, and hotels, and there is a need for them within sheltered housing accommodation where the elderly may not want or be able to go and sit in a salon.

It may be necessary to provide your own equipment. Because many products contain certain chemicals which can be harmful to the skin, hairdressers may find they have to wear protective gloves.

Hairdressing can be a lucrative area for the self-employed. While some conduct business from a spare room at home, others, who are able to drive, run a mobile hairdressing business. It is possible to rent a chair in a salon and pay the proprietor a weekly fee for the use of the facilities, thereby building up one's own clientele.

Qualifications and experience
Most people who return to hairdressing have generally had experience.

For those without prior knowledge some colleges keep

places on their full-time courses for mature students. These courses require examination passes in such subjects as English, art, maths and science.

Qualifications are changing at present, so it is necessary to check the situation with colleges. At present students may study for the City & Guilds (300) Basic Hairdressing Certificate. They may also study for the Hairdressing Training Board/C&G Foundation Certificate in Hairdressing (3010), which is designed for all new entrants into hairdressing. To achieve this certificate, candidates must satisfactorily complete 41 modules, displaying ability in various hairdressing skills. Students who are unable to complete the required number of modules are issued with a Certificate of Achievements.

Other hairdressing qualifications include the C&G Advanced Hairdressing Certificate (300-2) and the HTB/C&G Specialist Certificate in Hairdressing (3012, 3013) for those wishing to extend their hairdressing and supervisory skills.

Another training option is one of the privately run hairdressing schools where courses are more brief and intense. Tuition and examination fees are paid by the student. It may be advisable to check before embarking upon a privately run course as some of them offer qualifications which may not be recognised by employers. Some of the top schools run their own chain of salons; a 30-week intensive programme for beginners can cost between £2000 and £5000 at these world-renowned establishments.

It is usual after a period of training for hairdressers to work for a minimum of two years as 'improvers' prior to being regarded as experienced. Qualified hairdressers who have been out of employment for a time can take refresher courses at local day time colleges, evening classes or at private hairdressing schools.

Other jobs
Beauty Therapist; Sales Demonstrator; Manicurist

Contact
Write to managers at local sheltered accommodation where

71

the elderly might require a regular hairdresser; local hospitals.

As in all businesses the best way to arouse initial interest is to advertise. Hairdressers with young children at school or nursery may find it a good idea to pass cards around to other mothers, offering reasonable trimming costs for their children.

Hairdressing Training Board, Silver House, 17 Silver Street, Doncaster DN1 1HL; 0302 342837

Health Visitor

Hours	Several days per week
Pay	Full-time health visitors can earn £13,740–£15,900
Personal qualities	Patient; sympathetic; tactful; physically fit; able to put people at ease; not squeamish; happy to work alone; hold a driving licence

A health visitor generally works in the community advising people on a vast range of health matters. She maintains a close link with families, offering advice on the care of children, the handicapped and the elderly, and is often in attendance at child welfare and maternity clinics. It is her responsibility to form a relationship with clients, to identify their require-ments, and if necessary, arrange assistance.

She works closely with welfare and medical bodies such as social workers, doctors, district nurses, midwives, play-groups, day centres and residential establishments, and may be responsible for covering a certain designated area.

Health visitors with at least two years' full-time experience can take a field-work teacher course which will enable them to teach other health visitors. Further training may enhance their opportunities of moving into lecturing and there are courses available for those wishing to pursue a management career within the NHS.

Qualifications and experience
To become a qualified health visitor, an applicant must fulfil certain requirements: she must have had general nursing experience; possess the relevant midwifery/obstetric qualifications and experience; hold a degree or have undertaken a nurse/health visitor course. Failing these she should pass an entrance test.

Many general nursing training courses include an option in obstetric nursing, which may be an acceptable entry qualification into health visitor training.

There are several routes into health visiting: (a) For experienced general nurses with midwifery/obstetrics qualifications and experience there is a one-year post-registration course. Part-time courses last two years; (b) Graduates with related degrees are able to study for a modified post-registration course; (c) An RGN with the relevant obstetric qualification may take a degree course, which includes an option leading to health visitor registration.

The United Kingdom Central Council for Nursing, Midwifery and Health Visiting is totally responsible for training, examination and the issue of the professional certification of health visitors. Qualified health visitors must register with them in order to practise.

Other jobs
Nurse; Nursery Nurse; Auxiliary Assistant

Contact
Specialist publications in which vacancies appear: *Nursing Times, Nursing Standard, Midwife, Health Visitor, Community Nurse*

Write to: English National Board for Nursing, Midwifery and Health Visiting (address on page 151)

Health Visitor Association, 50 Southwark Street, London SE1 1UN; 071-378 7255

Hire Shop Owner

Hours	Flexible
Pay	Depends on the success of the venture
Personal qualities	An eye for a bargain; able to sew and undertake alterations; dexterous; fit; pleasant; well organised

There is always someone needing to hire something: it may be a wedding gown, a fancy dress outfit or even a piece of sports or garden equipment.

Running a hire business can be quite profitable. You receive payment for simply loaning out an item for a limited period, and any damage to the article which occurs while in the customer's possession is paid for by the customer. Such a venture may be organised from a spare room and for bulkier items, a garden shed or garage is ideal.

The hiring out of wedding dresses can be expanded to cover the bridesmaids' and bridegroom's outfits and possibly the entire wardrobe for parents.

If you decide to concentrate on hiring out fancy dress costumes, you have to make the initial outlay of buying them, or alternatively scouring antique shops for bits and pieces. Contact your local drama/theatre group which may be discarding costumes. They may let you have them for a small sum. There are always the local pages of *Exchange & Mart*, as well as newspapers and drama magazines.

Make sure that whatever you buy is perfectly safe or at least be confident of making it so. If in doubt, get a professional to check it over. Before hiring out the items make sure they are in first class condition, and check them again for any marks, stains or damage on their return.

Qualifications and experience

Anyone with an eye for a bargain could run their own hire business. Someone with experience as a sewing machinist or dressmaker would be well qualified to make their own costumes.

74

If you decide to hire out equipment you are responsible for ensuring that it is clean and fully operational before handing it over. Regular maintenance is important because you will only build up regular customers by offering a good service.

Two points to consider are: take out insurance to cover for accidents occurring to your property and against third party liability claims; check whether you are covered for running a business from your own home, and if not, take the appropriate action.

Other jobs
Alteration Hand; Garment Examiner; Shop Assistant; Market Stall Holder

Contact
Local Small Business Centre for further advice

To arouse interest, place an advertisement in the local press or have cards printed and distributed.

Home Help

Hours	Minimum 20 hours, maximum 25 hours per week
Pay	£3.33 per hour
Personal qualities	Able to get on with people; sympathetic; enjoys housework; patient; physically fit; cheerful; honest; reliable

A home help employed by the local Social Services is responsible for carrying out domestic duties for the elderly, handicapped or disabled people who are living alone.

The home help may go to one client for two hours per day twice a week, or a different client each day. Some home helps work seven days a week but these are usually special cases. Duties include: dusting and cleaning, perhaps making a light breakfast and washing the dishes up afterwards, making the bed; collecting a pension when required; shopping. In some circumstances home helps may be required to undertake domiciliary duties such as washing and dressing a person, as well as the other household chores.

There are certain jobs that home helps are not allowed to do for safety reasons. These may include washing windows, scrubbing floors or working in the garden.

Home helps normally work alone but occasionally a band of workers join together, possibly to clean a council house which has been left in a bad state by its previous tenant.

Spot checks are often undertaken by supervisors to ensure that work is being carried out satisfactorily.

There is plenty of opportunity for a home help to work privately. A hardworking, reliable housekeeper who comes in several days a week and does light housework duties is invaluable. You are advised to check the rate for cleaning in your area and then consider any other extra jobs you may be required to do, ie washing and ironing, preparing meals, etc, and base your fee on those, taking into account travelling costs incurred.

It is hard, tiring work and can be physically and mentally exhausting, listening to the sad stories some old people have to tell, but it also can be rewarding. The home help is often the only person they see from one day to the next, so those few hours spent in their company make a great deal of difference to them.

Qualifications and experience
No qualifications are required by a home help.

Other jobs
Cleaner; Laundry Service

Contact
Local Social Services

Housekeeper

Hours	Irregular hours, possibly shift system, weekend work or working two to three days per week
Pay	Fully trained housekeepers working full-time earn around £130 per week, but it largely depends on experience and employer
Personal qualities	Neat; meticulous; tactful; able to delegate and work well with others; well organised; reliable

A housekeeper can be employed in establishments such as a motel, guesthouse, hotel, local authority and private residential home, hall of residence, hospital or private residence. Her duties include supervising the work of the other domestic staff. She co-ordinates the activities of cleaners and inspects rooms to ensure they are clean and comfortable for guests; she reports faulty equipment to management, and is also responsible for ordering and issuing cleaning materials and linen.

A housekeeper works closely with other staff and, depending on the size of organisation, may be involved in management. Indeed, many housekeepers are responsible for paying the wages of domestic staff.

Qualifications and experience
Many employers prefer mature applicants, especially if they have had experience of working in the hotel/catering business. They like staff to have had a good standard of general education, preferably with some GCSE passes (A-C) in English, maths and a science subject. However, many employers set their own standards for applicants.

Many trainee housekeepers study for the City & Guilds 708 Certificate in Accommodation Services which is available at many colleges. There are no entry requirements, but many students take the one-year C&G 705 General Catering course which offers an introduction to the industry.

Colleges also run two-year full-time/sandwich courses leading to the BTEC National Diploma in Hotel, Catering and Institutional Operations or the BTEC National Certificate in Front Office and Accommodation Services. Entry to these courses is generally four GCSE passes (A–C) including English, a science subject and maths. On completion of a course, candidates are able to apply for posts as housekeepers. They are usually taken on as trainees, and training continues under the supervision of experienced staff.

Many employers accept applicants without qualifications to in-house training schemes which are on the job. Trainees usually attend college by day- or block-release to complete the relevant C&G or BTEC courses.

Other jobs
Room Attendant; Cleaner

Contact
Write to: National Examining Board for Supervisory Management, 76 Portland Place, London W1N 4AA; 071-580 3050

Hotel and Catering Trades Job Centre, 3 Denmark Street, London WC2H 8LR; 071-836 6622

Ironing

Hours	Approximately 10 hours per week, depending on how many jobs you get
Pay	£2–£3 per hour
Personal qualities	Physically fit; enjoys ironing; neat; able to drive an advantage

If you enjoy ironing, and some people do, then why not turn a pleasure into a business?

Many professional people and busy young mothers would gladly pay for such a service.

Charge clients an hourly rate and take into account time for collection and return. Do not forget to include the cost of labour, wear and tear on the iron, as well as the cost of electricity.

There are various points to be considered: some fabrics require different temperatures so make sure you check the labels before you begin; it may also be advisable to take out insurance for cover in the event of accidents.

Once you set up a string of clients perhaps you could arrange to collect the ironing on one day and deliver it the next. Never fail to turn up on the day promised.

Don't undervalue the job; it is hard work standing over an ironing board. Remember, doing it for the love of the family is one thing, but doing it to earn extra money can be a somewhat different matter.

Qualifications and experience
No qualifications are required.

Other jobs
Dry Cleaning Operator; Laundry Worker; Midday Supervisors; Kitchen Assistant

Contact
Advertise your ironing service by putting a postcard on notice-boards or in shop windows; place an ad in the local newspaper; tell friends and neighbours. There may be sheltered housing near you where elderly residents would appreciate such a service.

Kitchen Assistant

Hours	Variable – some jobs only available during the tourist season
Pay	£2.75 per hour

Personal qualities   Physically fit; tidy; reliable; impeccable personal hygiene

Kitchen assistants are employed in catering establishments to help the cook.

Her duties may include: preparing vegetables, cleaning and cutting up meats; general cleaning duties such as emptying waste bins, washing up and keeping the kitchen area tidy. She ensures that the kitchen is left immaculate and that will probably involve washing down work surfaces, floors, equipment, shelves and walls.

In some cases the assistant may be called upon to prepare soup or other simple dishes and make tea and coffee in the appropriate machines.

The kitchen assistant may have to assemble the cutlery and crockery before a meal is served, clean the silver platters and polish glasses. When deliveries of food are made, she may be called upon to lend a hand checking the consignment against the order and putting it away.

Qualifications and experience
No qualifications are required; ability and physical stamina are far more significant. However, experience in the catering trade is always a bonus.

It is usual for new recruits to be supervised by fully experienced assistants and shown the methods and routines of the particular organisation. Some organisations offer a career structure where it may be possible to train as a cook (see Cook).

Health and hygiene regulations may prevent sufferers from skin complaints from being accepted.

Other jobs
Bar Staff; Nursing Auxiliary; Home Help; Petrol Pump Attendant; Cleaner; Cook

Laboratory Technician

Hours	As agreed with employer
Pay	According to experience; full-time pay ranges from £10,000 to £15,300 in London
Personal qualities	Accurate; good eyesight; scientific approach; patient; responsible; able to work alone or as member of team; able to stand for long periods

Jobs exist in both the scientific and educational areas for laboratory technicians.

Their primary role is to help those working in laboratories and to carry out a range of duties, from setting up experiments to making sure that the equipment is operational. They may become involved in researching various projects and reporting results.

If working in a school or college the lab technician works closely with the science teacher setting up experiments, and making sure the equipment to be used is clean and works correctly. They sometimes assist the teacher in class. The technician is responsible for tidying up the lab, ordering new equipment, and repairing damaged items.

The areas in which lab technicians may be employed vary enormously and include schools, colleges, polytechnics and universities, the textile industry, the Ministries of Defence and Agriculture, Fisheries and Food, and local government.

The job may be unsuitable for those who have skin or respiratory problems because of the use of chemicals.

Qualifications and experience
Opportunities exist for the mature applicant, especially one who has some experience of working in a scientific environment. For those who are a little rusty and want to brush up on their skills some colleges organise 'return to science' courses.

Contacts
Write to: Food and Drink Federation, 6 Catherine Street,

London WC2B 5JJ; 071-836 2460, which runs a careers service for people wishing to become lab technicians

Institute of Science Technology, 73 Maygrove Road, London NW6 2RN; 071-328 9218

Laundry Worker

Hours	Approximately 20 hours per week
Pay	Varies according to training, experience, size of branch and turnover - minimum rate £1.80 per hour
Personal qualities	Tidy; neat; methodical; good eyesight; physically strong

The responsibilities of a laundry worker are similar to those of a dry cleaning worker. Depending on the size of company she could be asked to: check items when they come in and separate various materials before loading them into washing machines. When washed, items are usually dried and pressed by machines before being folded (a process normally done by hand). Finally, the laundry is packed ready for despatch.

Launderettes used by the general public are often open 24 hours a day. They are manned by staff working on a shift basis who make sure that the machines are working efficiently and sometimes do service washes.

As most commercial laundries concentrate on handling large bulky items, small hotels, old people's homes or restaurants may welcome a personal laundering service.

Once you have got several customers it could be to your advantage to devise a contract to ensure business is received on a regular basis. It is entirely up to you whether you decide to include ironing in your service, but you must charge extra for this.

Setting a realistic charge may prove rather difficult, but consider the time it takes; expenditure on electricity, cleaning materials (some large stores may give you discount if you buy in bulk), labour and petrol if you are expected to collect and return the laundry; maintenance of your own machine. Loads may need to be split as various items will require different washing machine programmes.

Qualifications and experience
No formal qualifications are required. However, most employers like staff to have a good standard of general education.

Other jobs
Ironing; Dry Cleaning Operator

Contact
Establish contact with small local businesses, place advertisements in shop windows and the local press, or get some cards printed and distributed

The Guild of Cleaners and Launderers (GCL), The Old Granary, Colwinston, Nr Cowbridge, South Glamorgan CF7 7NJ; 0446 774651

Library Assistant

Hours	Hours may be suited to the applicant
Pay	Public library assistants are paid on local authority scales. Private sector libraries have different rates
Personal qualities	Smart; methodical; patient; pleasant; able to communicate with people from all walks of life; a retentive memory

The role of a library assistant is to support and assist the librarian in her or his day-to-day duties.

Her job depends on the size of the library, but usually includes: dealing with returned books; issuing books; checking books for damage and putting them to one side for later repair; re-shelving books; checking cassettes, records and videos; sending out reminders for overdue books; assisting with enquiries from borrowers; attending to the daily arrival of newspapers and periodicals; helping with cataloguing and any other clerical duties.

Vacancies occur for assistants in public libraries, polytechnics, universities and privately run libraries, and there are occasional opportunities for assistants to go out on mobile libraries offering a service to the housebound or hospital patient.

Qualifications and experience

Although it is far easier for someone with experience as a library assistant to find employment in a library, mature applicants who show a sense of responsibility and the ability to learn might also be considered.

For those interested in becoming library assistants, training is done on the job but there are opportunities to attend college on a part-time basis for qualifications.

The City & Guilds (C&G 737) Library Assistant's Certificate course lasts for one year and is available on a part-time basis, intended for those who have been employed in library or information services. The examination comprises a practical assessment and two written papers.

There is another part-time course, the BTEC National Certificate in Business and Finance which is a two-year course providing an option in information or library work. This may be studied by day release or evening class. Qualifications required to study for the BTEC National Awards are four GCSEs (A–C).

For those unable to attend a registered centre the Local Government Training Board (in association with NALGO) organises a correspondence course.

Other jobs

Market Research; Interviewing; working in a bookshop

Contact

Local polytechnic or university libraries; County Council Offices

Write to: The Local Government Training Board, 4th Floor, Arndale House, The Arndale Centre, Luton LU1 2TS; 0582 451166

Mail Order Agent

Hours	Flexible
Pay	Commission based – usually 10 per cent in cash or 15 per cent if taken in goods
Personal qualities	Pleasant; numerate; neat handwriter; methodical; honest

A mail order agent works for an established firm and is responsible for selling goods from their catalogue to customers.

After the potential agent has made enquiries about running an agency the mail order company sends out a catalogue with the relevant paperwork explaining how to run the business side, ie ordering goods, payment methods, commission rates etc.

Some women prefer to keep the catalogue for members of the family only so that weekly repayments can be controlled.

Once orders have been made from the book, the agent fills in the order form and posts it off in the prepaid envelope. Alternatively, the agent may be able to phone through the order.

When the goods arrive she distributes them. The customer may keep the goods on approval before confirming whether she intends to keep them, but after that period, payment must begin.

It is the agent's responsibility to keep detailed records of the weekly payments in her statement ledger and in return issue and update the customer's payment card. The agent sends the money she has collected from her customers to the agency on a regular basis. How this is done is explained in the agent's starter information pack together with all the other necessary information.

Qualifications and experience
No training is required for such a job. Although the agent won't exactly become a millionaire, even with a lot of customers, it is a way of paying for those little extras that may otherwise be unaffordable.

Other jobs
Party Plan Agent; Retail Assistant

Contact
Mail order companies advertise in women's magazines and newspapers

Mail Order Assembler

Hours	May be shift work
Pay	£2.50–£4 per hour
Personal qualities	Quick; methodical; honest; meticulous

Mail order agencies employ staff to assemble and check off orders in their warehouse before being despatched to customers.

They usually work off a computer sheet and collect the required items from various points around the warehouse. Once the order has been checked with the supervisor it is then passed to the packers.

On the odd occasion when there is a shortage of the ordered goods the assembler may have to send a substitute. It is important that she monitors stock levels.

This job may be available only in certain areas.

Qualifications and experience
No qualifications are required.

Other jobs
Packer; Assembly Worker; Shelf Filler

Market Research Interviewer

Hours	Depends on the job – may be several days in one week/month; occasional weekend/ evening work
Pay	Varies – but not less than £20 per day plus travelling expenses
Personal qualities	Good listener; articulate; physically fit; smart; pleasant; able to put people at ease; resilient; confident

Companies conduct market research in order to monitor the success of their products.

The market research interviewer is employed to ask members of the public a selection of prepared questions relating to the company's product or service. This may be done by conducting personal interviews in the home of the consumer, at their place of work, or by interviewing people at random in the street, or in a particular location.

Government and public service bodies also commission market research to test reactions to a variety of issues.

Market research interviewing isn't usually a regular job (except in large cities), and when work is available, you may find yourself having to step in at short notice. In most cases interviewers are assigned their own area but if asked to go elsewhere travelling expenses will be paid.

Qualifications and experience

Although no formal qualifications are required to do this job, a good standard of general education with GCSE passes (A–C) in English and maths would be useful. Special training is usually required which involves several days at a conference centre or local hotel. Once the initial training and satisfactory supervision have been undertaken, interviewers are on their own, apart from the occasional visit from regional supervisors to check on their progress.

Other jobs

Merchandising; Shop work; Cold Canvassing

Contact

Write to: The Market Research Society, 15 Northburgh Street, London EC1V 0AH; 071-490 4911

Medical Herbalist

Hours	Sessional work one to two hours per day depending on number of patients
Pay	£5–£10 per consultation
Personal qualities	Patient; reassuring; interested in people; able to use own initiative; understanding; perceptive

Medical herbalism is one of the oldest methods of healing.

A fully trained medical herbalist treats patients by prescribing remedies which have been derived from plants. She finds out as much information about the patient as possible which includes medical history, family history, allergies, etc; this is done before a physical examination is carried out. She then considers the symptoms, makes a diagnosis and the treatment begins. This may be in the form of lotions, pills, ointments, poultices, tinctures, syrups or tablets. She may also advise the patient on a change of diet.

Many medical herbalists work within the NHS but others work for themselves.

Qualifications and experience

To practise students must first undertake training from one of the recognised bodies. Medical herbalism is regulated by two non-State bodies, which have different methods of training.

The National Institute of Medical Herbalists offers a four-year tutorial course, with both written and practical work supervised by a tutor; applicants are required to have a good educational background with GCSE passes (A–C) which should include chemistry, biology and English language. They also offer a four-year full-time course at their school of Herbal Medicine; applicants are required to have at least two GCSE passes (A–C) and preferably an A level in a science subject.

Other jobs

Naturopath; Homoeopath; Osteopath

Contact

Write to: The Institute for Complementary Medicine, 21 Portland Place, London W1N 3AF; 071-636 9543

The Registrar, School for Herbal Medicine and Phytotherapy, Buckstep Manor, Bodle Street Green, Hailsham BN27 4RJ

National Institute of Medical Herbalists, 9 Palace Gate, Exeter, Devon EX1 1JA (please send SAE)

Midday Supervisor

Hours   Approximately eight hours per week

Pay   £3 per hour

| Personal qualities | Pleasant; smart; clean; good with children; unflappable; patient |

Most schools employ midday supervisors during lunchtime. In a normal mainstream educational establishment their duties include: checking that the children have washed their hands before eating; being available in the dining hall when lunch is being served both to help the younger children and ensure there is no trouble. After lunch the supervisors usually superintend the children in the playground or encourage indoor activities in bad weather until it is time for school to resume.

If employed in a school where the children have special needs the supervisor may be required to sit down and help to feed the children.

Qualifications and experience
This is a job where personal attributes are far more important than academic qualifications. It is an ideal appointment for someone able to spare a few hours at lunchtime and who also enjoys the company of children.

Other jobs
Canteen Assistant; Classroom Assistant; Auxiliary Assistant; Escort; Clerk in a school; Kitchen Assistant; School Crossing Patrol

Contact
Local Education Office

Music Teacher

| Hours | If employed in a school could work staggered hours throughout the week. Private music teachers could work evenings and/or weekends |

Pay	Full-time teachers in England and Wales are paid on a scale commencing at £8500 plus extra payment for relevant experience. Part-time remuneration will be on a pro-rata basis. Private music teachers can charge whatever they feel the market will take
Personal qualities	Patient; musical; able to motivate students; good hearing; enthusiastic

A music teacher is employed in educational establishments and also privately, to teach the playing of musical instruments and/or give singing lessons to pupils of all ages.

Part of her job is to stimulate interest and instil enthusiasm for music in her pupils, helping them to develop individual talents and encouraging them to grow. She must also maintain progress records of her pupils and organise the school orchestra/choir or concerts.

Many music teachers change direction and go on to become music advisers for local authorities.

Qualifications and experience
To be accepted as a music teacher in a school it is important to possess 'recognised' teaching qualifications such as a BEd or Postgraduate Certificate in Education (PGCE) which requires full-time training. Teachers of adults do not require teaching qualifications.

Acceptance into specialist music courses requires high levels of skill in an instrument, together with academic qualifications.

Most colleges, universities and polytechnics will consider mature applicants who wish to take the BEd degree courses, and will occasionally accept them without the minimum requirements. However, they will need to demonstrate evidence of musical ability.

Other jobs
Performing Musician; Music Therapist

Contact
The Times Educational Supplement; music journals

Write to: UK Council for Music Education and Training, 13 Back Lane, South Luffenham, Oakham, Leicestershire LE15 8NQ; 0780 721115

The Associated Board of the Royal Schools of Music, 14 Bedford Square, London WC1B 3JG; 071-636 5400

Nanny

Hours	Flexible, largely depends on the requirements of the family. Unsocial hours may need to be worked
Pay	£2.50–£3.50 per hour
Personal qualities	Patient; sensitive to children's needs; reliable; healthy and strong; able to cope in emergencies; sense of humour

With more mothers returning to work after having their families there is an increasing demand for nannies and child minders. Some nannies live in, but many are employed on a daily basis, for one or more days a week.

A nanny is responsible for the day-to-day care of the children under her supervision. She looks after their practical needs, nurturing their abilities and encouraging independence. Her other duties involve preparing meals for the youngsters, washing their clothes, taking them out for walks or to local playgroups.

Qualifications and experience
Personal attributes are considered more important than formal qualifications but most employers expect applicants to possess a good standard of general education, together with some GCSE passes (A–C) including English. A mature

applicant without academic qualifications but with experience of working with children would be looked upon favourably.

It would be an advantage to possess the Nursery Nurse Examination Board Certificate (NNEB) which takes two years to achieve. Some colleges expect their applicants to possess several GCSE passes (A-C) before they accept them on to the course. The course itself involves academic study and practical experience in certain placements such as hospital or nurseries.

Other jobs
Nursery Nurse; Midday Supervisor; School Helper; Nursing Auxiliary; Mother's Help

Contact
For further information about the Certificate write to: National Nursery Examination Board, 8 Chequer Street, St Albans, Hertfordshire AL1 3XZ; 0727 47636

Naturopath

Hours	Sessions of one or two hours per day depending on how many patients you get
Pay	£5-£10 per session
Personal qualities	Tactful; dedicated; patient; reassuring; perceptive; able to encourage

A naturopath treats patients by natural methods, aiming to promote good health and relieve physical stress without the use of drugs or surgery. She discusses the case history of the patient and makes a physical examination, seeking the cause of the symptoms. After reaching a diagnosis, treatment can begin. It may take the form of diet, fasting, massage, hydrotherapy, psychotherapy etc.

Most naturopaths are employed in private practice and some work at health farms.

Qualifications and experience
To qualify as a naturopath applicants must attend a full-time training course which is available only at the British College of Naturopathy and Osteopathy. Entry requirements are three GCSE passes (A–C) which should include at least two from English language, maths and physics; and two A levels from chemistry and zoology or biology. Candidates must be in good health.

Students cover a range of pre-clinical subjects including biology, anatomy, nutrition, pathology etc; clinical studies include ophthalmology, orthopaedics, geriatrics etc. They are also required to prepare a thesis of between 7000 and 10,000 words and attend out-patient clinic sessions during the third and fourth years.

Graduates of the college are entitled to apply for membership of the British Naturopathic and Osteopathic Association.

The Incorporated Society of Registered Naturopaths offers another form of training in naturopathy whereby students are articled for two periods of training. The first one lasts one year, the second four years, working alongside experienced naturopaths and studying subjects relevant to natural cure.

Other jobs
Homeopath; Medical Herbalist; Osteopath

Contact
Write to: The Institute for Complementary Medicine, 21 Portland Place, London W1N 3AF; 071-636 9543

Incorporated Society of Registered Naturopaths, Kingston, The Coach House, 292 Gilmerton Road, Liberton, Edinburgh EH15 5UQ

British Naturopathic & Osteopathic Association & British College of Naturopathy & Osteopathy, 6 Netherhall Gardens, London NW3 5RR; 071-435 7830

Night Desk Clerk

Hours	Shift work, generally evenings 7pm–12pm working three to five days per week
Pay	Approximately £3.50 per hour
Personal qualities	Pleasant; clear speaker; good hearing; not nervous; knowledgeable about the area

A night desk clerk is usually employed by a taxi firm to run the office when the drivers are out on the road. Her job is to transmit calls to the taxi drivers via a linked radio. She is usually responsible for recording details of messages sent and received and for dealing with enquiries.

Training is given on the job. Applicants must be prepared to work unsocial hours.

Qualifications and experience
No formal qualifications are required. Employers expect staff to have a good general education but personal attributes are regarded as just as important. Good communication skills are essential.

Other jobs
Telephonist

Nurse

Hours	Shift work, with internal rotation – even for part-timers
Pay	RGNs can earn approximately £4.75 per hour
Personal qualities	Understanding; patient; physically fit; reassuring; sensitive; alert; sense of humour;

> able to act decisively; must not be
> squeamish

There are always opportunities for qualified nurses to work part time. Duties include: tending to the general care of patients, offering practical assistance with their comfort and treatment ie washing, dressing and feeding, making beds, emptying bedpans; assisting during operations and with other medical procedures such as injections or transfusions.

There are a number of different fields in which nurses may choose to work (maternity, geriatrics, surgical, psychiatric, ophthalmic, children's nursing, mentally handicapped, general hospital nursing, orthopaedic and so on).

Qualifications and experience

There is no statutory upper age limit for entry into nursing, and training schools use their discretion in accepting mature applicants. The maximum age to begin training for registered qualifications varies, but some schools accept applicants up to 45. If mature students do not have the equivalent of five GCSE passes (A-C) they may be able to sit the United Kingdom Central Council Educational Test.

Basic training to be a nurse takes over three years at schools of nursing which are affiliated to hospitals. Although the general syllabus is set by the UKCC, each school's training programme is approved by the National Boards which are in overall charge of nurse education. Training generally includes spending several weeks on each of the psychiatric, geriatric, obstetric and community wards, but the organisation of programmes varies from one hospital to another.

Generally applicants apply through a central clearing house, and as there is still no course comparison material, it is in the nurses' interest to apply directly to several colleges, and visit them before making a decision.

First level training - registered nursing entry qualifications are generally five GGSE passes (A-C) including English and at least one science subject. Some schools may require A levels. A pass in an approved educational test (set by the UKCC, taken together with the applicant's own suitability for the job, track record, potential etc) may also be acceptable. Graduates may train for the general part of the register by undertaking either the three-year Registered General Nursing course or a shortened postgraduate RGN.

Refresher courses are available for nurses wishing to return to the profession. See *Nursing As A Second Career* by Margaret Korving (Kogan Page) 1990.

Other jobs
Nursing Auxiliary; Care Worker; Occupational Therapist; Speech Therapist; Social Worker

Contact
National Board for Nursing, Midwifery and Health Visiting Resource & Careers Services (address on page 151)

Nursing Auxiliary

Hours	Various shift systems
Pay	National Health Service salaries for full-timers range from £4750–£6090
Personal qualities	Reliable; sympathetic; cheerful; pleasant; physically fit; not squeamish; tolerant

A nursing auxiliary works in a hospital or clinic assisting nurses in the care and treatment of patients. She undertakes the basic nursing duties such as: making beds, issuing and emptying bedpans, keeping wards tidy, helping patients to feed, wash and dress themselves, and she may also apply and remove dressings.

Her general duties include: preparing and giving out drinks, sorting laundry, doing errands and sometimes escorting patients to other parts of the hospital. She arranges lockers for new admissions, prepares patients for the operating theatre and keeps a general check on patients, informing medical staff of changes.

There is a one-year training programme with five levels of

skill; recruits receive classroom tuition on first aid and infection control, instruction and practice in bedmaking, bedbathing, mouth care and hygiene etc. Ward training is usually done by experienced staff.

Opportunities exist for nursing auxiliaries who would like further training to enable them to read temperatures, take urine tests and change bandages.

Qualifications and experience
No formal qualifications are required but employers expect staff to have a good standard of general education. Some hospitals require applicants to take a medical examination and some set an entrance examination.

Other jobs
Care Assistant; Operating Department Assistant; Ward Orderly; Occupational Therapy Helper; Physiotherapy Helper; Nurse

Contact
National Board for Nursing, Midwifery and Health Visiting Resource & Careers Services (address on page 151)

Occupational Therapist

Hours	Depend very much on the employer; many occupational therapists work two to three days a week; others may work five mornings or afternoons
Pay	NHS salaries commence at £9225 full time with increments according to grade
Personal qualities	Resourceful; sympathetic; patient; cheerful; physically fit and strong; observant; able to communicate with people of all ages and to inspire confidence

An occupational therapist treats patients who have suffered a temporary or permanent physical or mental handicap/illness, usually by planning programmes of work and recreational activities to hasten recovery.

Her duties will vary according to the age and medical condition of the patient but generally include: teaching recreational activities such as painting and craftwork to the bed-ridden, elderly or disabled, thereby giving them an interest and a sense of achievement; arranging social activities and encouraging patients to socialise with others; finding suitable employment for the disabled or injured. At all times she must maintain records of her patients' progress.

Most occupational therapists work for the NHS in a hospital alongside other members of the medical team, but occasionally in the local authority social services departments and in homes.

Qualifications and experience

Many mature people train to become occupational therapists and those with nursing or physiotherapy qualifications may find it possible to take a shortened two-year diploma course. Mature students who show evidence of recent academic study and scientific ability will find that many schools waive their educational requirements.

Training is for three years full time. It prepares candidates for the diploma of the College of Occupational Therapists, (DipCOT).

The subjects covered in the course include: the pathology of conditions which can be treated by occupational therapy and practical skills and techniques, anatomy, physiology, psychology and psychiatry. Part of the course is practical work at a hospital under the supervision of a qualified occupational therapist. It is permissible for UK graduates in such subjects as psychology, biology or sociology to take a reduced two-year training course. Degree courses are offered by six colleges in Britain.

The minimum qualifications for entry are: six GCSE passes (A-C) including one, often two A levels; subjects should include English and a science, preferably biology. Entry requirements differ from school to school, so it is advisable that applicants consult prospectuses. Personal qualities are very important and are assessed at interview.

Other jobs
Speech Therapist

Contact
Write to: The College of Occupational Therapists, 6-8 Marshalsea Road, London SE1 1HL; 071-357 6480

Orthoptist

Hours	Several days per week
Pay	Full-time orthoptists employed in the NHS start off by earning £9225. Those in private practice earn slightly more
Personal qualities	Reassuring; sympathetic; able to communicate with people of all ages; capable of understanding scientific jargon

An orthoptist works closely with the ophthalmic surgeon. She assists him or her in the diagnosis and treatment of squints and other sight-related problems. If surgery is not required the orthoptist is responsible for devising a plan to re-educate the eye muscles and monitor the patient's progress. If surgery is required, she works closely with the ophthalmic surgeon, offering information before and after the operation.

Much of her work is with young children, assessing their visual ability. She also works with the mentally and physically handicapped, the elderly, sufferers of debilitating diseases such as multiple sclerosis and those who may have suffered strokes etc.

Most orthoptists are employed in NHS hospitals, but opportunities also exist in private practice and in the education service.

100

Qualifications and experience

Although there is a preponderance of young entrants to this profession, it is acceptable for mature entrants to return after a career break provided they have kept up to date.

Training involves a three-year diploma course combining practical and theoretical studies. To practise within the NHS orthoptists must be state registered, which may only be done if they hold the Diploma of the British Orthoptic Council.

There are many part-time/full-time/correspondence courses leading to the diploma. Entry requirements: two A levels and five GCSE passes (A–C) including English, one science and maths.

For those interested in teaching the two higher qualifications are: the Orthoptic Demonstrator's Certificate and Orthoptic Teacher's Certificate.

Other jobs

Dispensing Optician

Contact

Specialist publications in which vacancies appear: The British Orthoptic Society produces a journal, *Dispensing Optics*

Write to: The Association of British Dispensing Opticians, 6 Hurlingham Business Park, Sullivan Road, London SW6 3DU; 071-736 0088

British Orthoptic Society, Tavistock House North, Tavistock Square, London WC1H 9HX; 071-387 7992

Packer

Hours	Approximately 20 hours per week, possibly worked on a shift basis
Pay	£2.50–£3 per hour
Personal qualities	Careful; safety conscious; physically fit; neat;

> co-operative; methodical; able to work alone
> or as member of team

A packer who is employed in a factory will generally pack goods in crates/boxes/cartons for transportation, sorting out the articles and packing them securely and neatly in order to avoid damage. Her other duties may involve labelling and weighing the container.

Promotion prospects are few, although some packers do take on supervisory appointments or move into quality control work. Training varies according to the employer.

Qualifications and experience

Employers expect staff to have a good standard of general education and personal qualities are considered important. Many employers set an aptitude test, used to determine the individual's practical ability for the type of work.

Firms frequently organise induction training where new recruits are introduced to the company and its policies. This will cover such subjects as medical facilities, conditions of employment, etc. This training is usually undertaken on the premises.

Other employers offer instruction for a few hours or two to three weeks, depending on the job.

Other jobs

Quality Control Inspector; Assembler; Sewing Machinist

Party Entertainer

Hours	An hour or two a week depending on the number of party bookings
Pay	Expect to earn £25–£40 per party – but obviously this varies with the area and entertainment value of the act

Personal qualities   Pleasant; outgoing personality; adaptable,
                        able to encourage audience participation;
                        enthusiastic; self-confident

Can you juggle, can you sing or mime, can you dress up as a
clown and make everyone laugh? Perhaps your forte lies in
playing an instrument, or putting on a Punch and Judy show?
Wherever your talents lie there is sure to be employment for
you, not only at children's birthday parties but any other
function where entertainment is required.

To arouse interest in your party entertainment act, advertise your services in the local newspaper, have some posters
printed and distribute them around local playgroups or
schools, ask the local library if they would display a poster on
the notice board and place a postcard in shop windows.

A fun job for people who enjoy sharing their talent with
others.

Qualifications and experience
The only experience you require for such a job is talent, and a
way of communicating your enthusiasm to others.

Petrol Pump Attendant

Hours   Shift work. Covering bank holidays or
                        weekends

Pay   £2–£2.50 per hour

Personal qualities   Pleasant; polite; helpful; able to deal with
                        money; trustworthy; security conscious;
                        physically fit; reliable; able to work alone

Garages employ petrol pump/forecourt attendants. Duties
include: serving petrol and/or operating the console, acting
as cashier, operating the till and handling cash or credit
cards, selling car accessories and drinks etc. She is also

responsible for the day-to-day running of the petrol station, checking and signing when new supplies of petrol are brought in; she maintains a check on stock levels and is responsible for re-ordering supplies. She may have to ensure that the forecourt is kept clean and assist customers whenever required. In some garages she will check the oil, water and battery and adjust tyre pressures.

Training is usually undertaken on the job under the eye of an experienced attendant. Trainees are shown how to operate the petrol pumps in an attended station, operate the console in a self-service station and to deal with the cash register. They are also instructed on various other tasks such as changing till rolls, balancing cash at the end of the day etc, company policy on credit cards, cheques and customers' accounts.

Qualifications and experience
No formal qualifications are required. Most employers expect applicants to have a good standard of general education and may require them to take a simple arithmetic test at the interview.

Other jobs
Checkout Operator; Retail Assistant; Shelf Filler

Contact
Keep an eye on the local garages

Pharmacist

Hours	Several days per week or five mornings/afternoons
Pay	Qualified pharmacists employed full time in industry can earn from £12,500 to £20,000; those employed by the NHS earn from £10,300 to £25,000. During the pre-registration year they can earn about £8000.

Personal qualities   Accurate; interested in science; clear thinking; responsible; able to work as member of team or alone

A pharmacist issues drugs and medicines, which have usually been prescribed by a doctor, to the public. This may involve making up prescriptions or dispensing ready-made preparations. She is responsible for ensuring that poisonous substances are registered, stocks are correctly stored and replenished as and when necessary. She is also able to offer advice on the correct use and side effects of certain drugs, and to discuss the treatment of minor complaints, often acting as an intermediary between doctor and patient.

Opportunities exist in hospitals, industry and within a pharmacy.

Qualifications and experience
Educational establishments often encourage older applicants by reducing entry requirements, although the ability to study to a high level must be proved. Whatever the age of applicants, the same training route has to be followed.

Before any pharmacist is able to practise in a hospital, within some areas of industrial pharmacy or in a pharmacy, she must first register as a pharmacist, which leads to Membership of the Royal Pharmaceutical Society of Great Britain. Registration is only available to those who hold a degree in pharmacy and have also completed a one-year period of pre-registration experience under the supervision of a fully qualified pharmacist.

Entry requirements for a degree course are two or three A levels, one of which should be chemistry and/or another science subject and maths; with three GCSE passes (A–C) which should include physics/biology and maths. Candidates should consult university and polytechnic prospectuses and the Pharmaceutical Society for full details.

Degree courses, which usually last three years, are run at several establishments throughout the country. Courses vary, but they normally involve the study of several pharmaceutical sciences including: the origin and make-up of drugs, uses and side effects of drugs and medicines, aspects of medicines used in pharmaceuticals, and the practice of pharmacy. Following on from this students generally follow a pre-registration year which provides them with a valuable look into working in pharmacy.

Other jobs
Dentist; Laboratory Technician; Pharmacy Technician

Contact
Specialist publications in which vacancies appear: *Nature, New Scientist, The Pharmaceutical Journal*

Write to: The Royal Pharmaceutical Society of Great Britain, 1 Lambeth High Street, London, SE1 7JN; 071-735 9141

The Association of British Pharmaceutical Industry, 12 Whitehall, London SW1A 2DY; 071-930 3477

The National Pharmaceutical Association, Mallinson House, 40–42 St Peter's Street, St Albans, Hertfordshire AL1 3NP (enclose SAE)

Pharmacy Technician

Hours	May work on a rota basis to provide a locally agreed dispensing service
Pay	NHS rates for full-time qualified pharmacy technicians are about £8000
Personal qualities	Meticulous; scientifically minded; methodical; alert; able to get on with people; observant

A pharmacy technician may be employed in a hospital or a chemist shop. Under the supervision of the pharmacist she assists with the preparation and dispensing of medicines, helps to make up the prescription, measure out liquid, count tablets etc. She checks stock levels and is often involved in invoicing and ordering; if employed in a retail chemist she will also sell items over the counter.

A pharmacy technician cannot become a pharmacist without the necessary study (see Pharmacist). Some, however, diversify and progress into marketing with drug companies. If employed in a hospital, there is possible promotion to senior technician after several years' study. Training is done on the job, supplemented by part-time study for one of the many recognised qualifications.

Qualifications and experience
Employers expect staff to have a good standard of general education and also several GCSE passes (A–C) including English, a science subject and maths.

The Society of Apothecaries Pharmacy Technicians' Certificate is a two-year part-time day release or evening course. Students who gain the certificate can take a further one-year day release course leading to the BTEC National Certificate. Candidates require four GCSE passes (A–C) including English, maths and a science.

The BTEC Certificate in Pharmaceutical Science is a two/three-year part-time day-release course directed at those currently employed in the retail pharmacy – there are minimum entry qualifications. Students who have some GCSE passes (A–C) may be exempt from part of the course. A correspondence course is also available from the National Pharmaceutical Association.

Other jobs
Pharmacist; Laboratory Technician

Contact
The National Pharmaceutical Association, Mallinson House, 40–42 St Peter's Street, St Albans, Hertfordshire AL1 3NP (enclose SAE)

The Pharmaceutical Society of Great Britain, 1 Lambeth High Street, London SE1 7JN; 071-735 9141

The Society of Apothecaries, Apothecaries Hall, Blackfriars Lane, London EC4V 6EJ; 071-236 1189

Photographer

Hours	Freelances can arrange hours to suit, subject to clients' requirements
Pay	Salaries vary greatly and start off low, but full-time social and wedding photographers with experience can earn about £10,000, whereas a medical photographer's rates range from £4743 to £6751 when trained
Personal qualities	Creative; confident; fast worker; determined; patient; good eyesight

Photography covers many areas including: taking social photographs for private individuals; taking photographs of properties for sale for estate agents; the advertising world; fashion; industry; science; forensic; medicine; and there is the whole world of press and photo-journalism which may well involve working erratic hours. Many photographers dabble in everything while some specialise in one particular area.

Qualifications and experience
Although photography is dominated by younger people, mature applicants without qualifications may be allowed on to courses provided they show ability. There are many photography courses available but entry largely depends on the person's age, experience and ambitions.

Many people train for photography on a part-time basis while in employment; others study an art and design course which specialises in photography, and some undertake a full-time photography course leading to a City and Guilds qualification. There are no set entry requirements, although some colleges expect candidates to hold GCSE passes including English, maths, art, and a science. Students in employment are able to take the C&G over three years. Full-time courses are also available.

Other qualfications leading to a career in photography include the BTEC National Diploma or HND or a degree qualification.

Some hospitals take trainees on without formal training but applicants are required to have five GCSE passes (A–C) including a science and English language. Courses are usually on a part-time basis. For further details write to Institute of Medical Illustrators.

Many private colleges organise full- and part-time courses, which range from a few days to several years. There are correspondence courses in photography. City and Guilds qualifications are also available.

Contact
Specialist publications in which vacancies appear: *The Journalist; Nature; Industrial and Commercial Photographer; British Journal of Photography; New Scientist; Design; Photographic Weekly*

Write to: British Institute of Professional Photography, Fox Talbot House, Amwell End, Ware, Hertfordshire SG12 9HN; 0920 4011

Institute of Medical Illustrators, Bank Chambers, 48 Onslow Gardens, London SW7 3AH (SAE required)

Physiotherapist

Hours	Could involve working five mornings/ afternoons per week. Largely depends on the employer's requirements
Pay	Salaries for full-time NHS physiotherapists range from £9460 for the newly qualified to about £20,000
Personal qualities	Patient; physically fit and strong; firm; sympathetic; cheerful; able to inspire confidence; tactful

A physiotherapist rehabilitates people who have suffered

some physical disability as a result of illness, injury or the onset of old age. She helps to return the patient to as near normal function of body and limbs as possible, encouraging independence and improving mobility.

To do this a physiotherapist uses many methods of treatment based on movement and manipulation, including massage, electrotherapy, ultrasound, and heat treatments. Consulting other medical staff she studies each individual patient's case history before the relevant treatment is administered. A physiotherapist works with people of all ages from babies to the elderly and maintains a progress report for each patient.

Apart from hospitals a physiotherapist could find part-time work in sports and health clubs or gymnasia.

For those fully qualified physiotherapists with three years' clinical experience, opportunities exist to study for the Certificate in Education and Diploma for Teachers of Physiotherapists. Some physiotherapists train to become clinical specialists while others may move into management positions.

Qualifications and experience

Although many schools welcome mature students because they take into account experience, educational qualifications and ability to study at degree level, mature applicants aged over 35 may find it rather difficult to get on to a training course.

Many colleges welcome mature applicants and will take into consideration any educational qualifications and experience. They will usually require some evidence of ability to study at degree level.

The minimum educational requirements for entry into training are five GCSE passes (A–C) including two science subjects and English, and two A levels. A-level grades should be in academic subjects and a biological science is preferred. As an alternative to A levels, a BTEC National Diploma in science would be considered.

Before being accepted into training, applicants must prove they have taken part in physical education activities and will be required to pass a medical. Some schools require a minimum height for students of 5'2" (1.6m). The ability to swim is useful.

Students take an approved degree or diploma course which makes them eligible for membership of the Chartered Society of Physiotherapy (MCSP) and for State Registration. National Health Service employees must be State Registered. Courses last three or four years full time. Details are available from the Chartered Society of Physiotherapists.

Courses are a combination of practical and theoretical work and cover: pathology, anatomy, physiology, physics, behavioural science, theory and practice of therapeutic movement, and manipulation.

Other jobs
Osteopath; Physiotherapy Helper; Occupational Therapist; Chiropodist; Chiropractor; Nurse

Contact
Write to: The Chartered Society of Physiotherapy, 14 Bedford Row, London WC1R 4ED; 071-242 1941

Physiotherapy Helper

Hours	Approximately 18 hours per week
Pay	£2797–£3000, based on the above hours
Personal qualities	Patient; reliable; helpful; physically fit and strong; pleasant; sympathetic; able to encourage people; able to work as part of team

Physiotherapy helpers work in hospitals assisting the fully qualified physiotherapists in the assessment, treatment and rehabilitation of the patients. Their duties involve taking care of patients as they arrive, offering assistance when they are dressing and undressing; helping patients with their exercises; preparing the equipment required for various types of treatment and ensuring the apparatus and work area are kept clean and tidy.

Training is usually given under the supervision of a qualified physiotherapist. Opportunities exist for those who wish to qualify as a physiotherapist.

Qualifications and experience
No formal qualifications are required although employers would expect applicants to have a good standard of general education. Experience working in a hospital, particularly with the elderly or the disabled, would be an advantage.

Other jobs
Nursing Auxiliary; Care Assistant; Nurse

Contact
Local Hospitals

Write to: The Chartered Society of Physiotherapy, 14 Bedford Row, London WC1R 4ED; 071-242 1941

Production Worker

Hours	Approximately 25 hours per week, possibly worked on a shift basis
Pay	£3.50–£4.50 per hour
Personal qualities	Physically strong; reliable; quick; able to follow instructions; good time-keeper; able to work as member of team; dexterous

The manufacturing industry employs many workers on a part-time basis to undertake the routine tasks involved in producing manufactured goods.

Although duties obviously vary according to the industry in which production workers are employed, they generally include: weighing and mixing materials, operating or monitoring machines, assembling and packing articles or working on a conveyor belt. Some firms move operators around to make those routine tasks a little more interesting and varied. Being a production worker can often involve remaining in one position throughout your shift which can be tiring and monotonous.

Promotion prospects are fairly limited although some people may progress to supervisory positions or move into quality control work.

Training for the job generally varies according to the employer and the type of product manufactured.

Qualifications and experience
Most employers would expect their staff to have a good general education with some GCSE passes (A–C) in practical subjects or a science. Personal qualities are also considered important. Many employers set an aptitude test, particularly where the work requires manual dexterity or the ability to follow detailed instructions.

Many firms organise induction training where new recruits are introduced to the company's policy, practices and products. The subjects covered are usually conditions of employment, medical facilities, staff welfare and health and safety matters. This training may be held in the firm's training centre or consist of a brief introductory talk and tour around the factory.

In some jobs the employer gives new recruits instruction for a few hours or two to three weeks, depending on the job. Some employers send operatives to study on a part-time basis at technical college. Training may be through day-/block-release and can lead to relevant qualifications awarded by the City and Guilds of London Institute or college/regional boards. Subjects covered include: operating equipment and machinery, instrumentation and production/process techniques and safety or emergency procedures.

Other jobs
Packer; Quality Control Inspector; Assembler; Sewing Machinist

113

Receptionist

Hours	Approximately 20 hours per week
Pay	£2.50–£3 per hour
Personal qualities	Confident; outgoing personality; helpful; articulate; pleasant; good telephone manner; numerate; efficient; smart

A receptionist is the first representative of an organisation a customer meets on entering the company. It is therefore essential that she projects a favourable image.

Where a receptionist works will dictate her responsibilities, but these generally include: greeting people upon arrival; asking who they are and whether they have an appointment; dealing with queries; taking messages. She could also operate the telephone switchboard, undertake filing, type, sort and distribute in-coming mail and frank out-going mail, handle cash, do simple bookkeeping, collect cash from the bank and undertake other clerical duties.

Most receptionists are trained on the job, learning how to work the switchboard, deal with awkward customers, and maintain records.

Qualifications and experience
Most employers like their receptionists to have a good general education and hold some GCSE passes (A–C); occasionally typing is required. Mature applicants are looked upon favourably, especially those who have had some work experience.

There are full-time pre-employment courses, lasting one year: the Royal Society of Arts (RSA) Certificate in Office Practice Stage 1, Certificate in Reception Skills, Diploma in Reception Skills Stage 1, City and Guilds Certificate 716 in General Reception, BTEC general awards.

Those wishing to become a medical receptionist should contact the Association of Medical Secretaries, Practice Administrators and Receptionists (AMSPAR) for details of their courses. The subjects covered include: reception duties; switchboard operation, office machinery and technology,

114

internal office communication; communication skills: record and filing systems, note taking, bookkeeping, typing; and background information: business organisation, business studies, banking, insurance.

Other jobs
Clerk; Secretary

Contact
Association of Medical Secretaries, Practice Administrators & Receptionists (AMSPAR) Tavistock House North, Tavistock Square, London WC1H 9LN; 071-388 2648

Retail Assistant

Hours	Approximately 20 hours per week
Pay	£2.70 per hour
Personal qualities	Smart; punctual; pleasant; polite; clear voice; numerate; trustworthy; fit

There are many differing retail outlets, varying in size from corner shop to huge hypermarket. The duties of a sales assistant will vary according to the size and type of shop but basically include: assisting customers in their choice of goods; advising on colour and style; wrapping goods and receiving payment, which may be by cash, cheque or credit card.

The size of the retail outlet will determine what other responsibilities she is given such as stock control, ensuring shelves are clean and tidy, and checking that items are correctly priced. She may be required to dust floors and clean windows too.

In large department, chain or multiple stores it is usual for new recruits to be trained in a classroom or an office, supplemented by a course of off-the-job training. Trainees are taught about the products they sell, company systems, pricing policy, company policy on cheques and credit cards and are shown around the retail outlet. In smaller retail outlets topics are generally covered less formally and more of the training is undertaken in the sales area.

Qualifications and experience
There are many qualifications for which one can study: (a) The BTEC National Certificate in Distribution, a two-year part-time study course for which entry requirements are four GCSE passes (A–C); (b) The Higher National Certificate offers a Certificate in Distribution to trainee managers, and the minimum entry requirements are: one A level plus three GCSE passes (A–C); (c) The Post-experience Certificate in Management Studies is a part-time course designed for those with A levels who possess relevant experience; (d) The College for the Distributive Trades offers a wide range of BTEC awards and entry requirements range from none to A levels and practical experience. The Pitman Examinations Institute also runs relevant courses.

Other jobs
Receptionist; Checkout Operator; Petrol Pump Attendant; Store Demonstrator; Beauty Consultant; Window Dresser; Merchandiser; Cashier

Contact
The National Examining Board for Supervisory Management (NEBSS), 76 Portland Place, London W1N 4AA; 071-580 3050

Write to: Pitman Examinations Institute, Catteshall Manor, Catteshall Lane, Godalming, Surrey GU7 1UU; 04868 5311

Retail Merchandiser

Hours   Flexible – 15 hours per week

Pay   £3 per hour plus expenses

Personal qualities	Smart; pleasant; numerate; eye for detail; able to work alone; capable of communicating with people at all levels; able to drive

A retail merchandiser is employed to travel around various outlets within an assigned area to check on the sales of particular products.

Their other responsibilities include: ensuring the product is displayed to the best advantage; checking on supply figures and stock levels; introducing new products to the management and liaising with the manager over any problems. She may also fill shelves when the need arises.

Although generally working alone, the merchandiser is in contact with a supervisor whom she can contact in need of any emergencies or problems. Training is done on the job.

Qualification and experience
No formal qualifications are required; however, employers expect their staff to have a good standard of general education and it is always useful to have some GCSE passes (A–C). Previous merchandising or sales experience is also an advantage.

Other jobs
Interviewer

Room Attendant

Hours	Approximately 14 hours per week. Vacancies for temporary work exist throughout the tourist season
Pay	£2.40 per hour
Personal qualities	Tidy; honest; polite; neat; physically fit; reliable; pleasant

Hotels, guest houses, halls of residence, motels and other residential establishments employ hotel room attendants. Their duties include: cleaning and tidying the bedrooms, making beds, changing linen, cleaning floors, dusting furniture, emptying wastepaper bins, removing dirty tea trays and glasses, cleaning ash trays. They must also clean the bathrooms, wash or vacuum the floors, clean baths and wash basins, replenish room supplies.

In some hotels attendants serve early morning tea, distribute mail, serve light meals and collect guests' laundry and dry cleaning. Occasionally, when all the bedroom cleaning has been done, room attendants may clean corridors, staircases, and wash down walls.

Training is undertaken on the job with instruction from the housekeeper or an experienced member of staff. Trainees are taught how to make beds and other domestic skills in accordance with hotel procedure. Some hotels run short induction courses or give instruction on health and safety.

Qualifications and experience
No formal qualifications are required but employers expect their staff to have a good standard of general education. It is a job where personal attributes are regarded as important.

Opportunities exist for room attendants to study for the City and Guilds Specific Skill Schemes such as the 700–2 for room service staff.

Although training is generally undertaken at the place of work the Hotel and Catering Training Board (HCTB) recommend courses lasting for six to eight weeks with subjects including practical cleaning skills, care and use of tools and equipment, working practice and procedures, hygiene and health etc. Trainees complete a course work assessment, and are tested in theory and practical skills. Successful candidates are awarded with a certificate.

Other jobs
Nursing Auxiliary; Kitchen Assistant; Home Help; Window Cleaner; Dry Cleaning Operator; Laundry Worker; Ironing

Contact
Hotel and Catering Trades Job Centre, 3 Denmark Street,
London WC2H 8LR; 071-497 2047

School Crossing Patrol

Hours	Usually eight hours per week on a split-day basis
Pay	£2.96 per hour
Personal qualities	Physically fit; decisive; pleasant; able to handle children

Traditionally known as the Lollipop Lady/Man, this highly responsible role is important to the welfare and safety of children going to and from school. People undertaking such a job are employed by the local council, to ensure that children are escorted safely across the road at certain locations, designated by the council. These sites are usually close to schools or in areas of heavy traffic.

Not only is a Lollipop Lady responsible for guiding youngsters safely across the road, but she also has to ensure that they behave in a reasonable manner at the kerbside; one push from a friend could result in an accident.

Training usually consists of working alongside an experienced colleague for a few days, after which the Lollipop Lady is left to work alone with the occasional surprise visit from a supervisor to ensure that duties are being carried out satisfactorily.

Qualifications and experience
No formal qualification or experience is required. Mature applicants are looked upon favourably.

Other jobs
Traffic Research; Midday Supervisor; Auxiliary Worker

Secretary

Hours	20–25 hours per week. Much temporary work is available through agencies
Pay	£3.50 per hour
Personal qualities	Efficient; reliable; punctual; smart; cheerful; courteous; neat; flexible; good telephone manner; able to work with people of all ages

A good secretary is often described as being indispensable to her boss. Her duties generally include: answering telephone calls, receiving visitors, opening correspondence, taking dictation and transcribing it as letters or reports etc. Some draw up agendas before a meeting, others sit in on meetings and take minutes, then type them up afterwards.

She may have to make travel arrangements, plan receptions and organise conferences; liaise with other secretaries, deal with petty cash, handle bookkeeping duties, keep files, and be familiar with all the office equipment including word processors, telex and fax machines, photocopiers and franking machines.

Some secretaries specialise in a particular area such as law, knowledge of a foreign language, or medicine; others supervise several typists or clerks in a large office and many take some of the workload from their bosses. Other secretaries prefer to change direction and take teaching posts in commercial and secretarial colleges after obtaining a teaching certificate.

Much of the training a secretary undertakes is on the job, once she has obtained the basic skills.

Qualifications and experience
A mature secretary, especially one with past office/secretarial experience, is regarded as an asset to any firm. Refresher courses are available for those who feel their secretarial skills are a little rusty. There are also courses in word processing for those with typing experience. Some secretarial agencies run them.

The most important qualifications for a secretary are that she is able to type neatly and accurately at speeds between 40 and 70 wpm either from a tape or shorthand, and a shorthand speed of approximately 100 wpm. Most students train to become secretaries by taking full-time courses after school. Advanced secretarial courses are available for students with A levels or degrees. Available courses: (a) For graduates or school leavers with A levels, three to nine-month courses in which basic secretarial skills are taught; (b) Courses lasting six to twenty-four months are available for students with GCSE passes (A–C); (c) Students with lower grade GCSE passes may attend one to two-year part-time courses which could ultimately lead on to clerical/typing jobs and after gaining experience, secretarial work; (d) For those with few or no qualifications there are part-time, day release or evening class courses. These lead to a variety of qualifications which are accepted by the commercial world, eg the Royal Society of Arts, Pitman Examinations Institute, London Chamber of Commerce and Industry and the BTEC. Students are required to take speed tests in shorthand and typing or audio-typing, and to those successful in passing, a certificate or diploma is awarded.

When choosing a course opt for the one which offers a wide range of qualifications and tuition.

Other jobs
Court Reporter; Receptionist; Word Processing Operator

Contact
Write to: Institute of Qualified Private Secretaries, 126 Farnham Road, Slough, Berkshire SL1 4XA; 0753 22395. Send SAE.

Sewing Machinist

Hours	A fixed number of hours worked over a week and opportunities for home-working
Pay	Approximately £2.25 per hour
Personal qualities	Good eyesight; quick; neat; accurate; adept; able to work alone or as member of team

A sewing machinist can be employed in a busy factory which turns out a vast quantity of clothes every day, in a small manufacturing factory which deals with more specialised items, or work for herself from home. In whichever field she works, her job usually entails sitting at a sewing machine and sewing up part or the whole of a garment or article. Maintenance of the machine may also be her responsibility. She may be employed on a freelance basis, being called on when necessary. Vacancies often appear in local newspapers.

It is also possible for machinists to run their own business, perhaps making curtains or duvet covers, offering an alteration service or making wedding dresses, but it is advisable to check out the market beforehand to become fully acquainted with what is needed.

A machinist could train to become a supervisor in charge of a team of machinists, or alternatively a garment examiner. It is quite usual for a fully experienced machinist to become an instructor, or change direction and go into quality control.

A lot of companies have a particular section where new recruits work for several weeks learning how to operate a machine. During this training period they usually earn a basic weekly wage. Once sufficiently experienced, a machinist will go on to the factory floor on piecework rates. Many companies send trainees on a day-release course which leads ultimately to the City and Guilds 460. This course offers students an overview of the industry rather than specific skill training and there are opportunities also to specialise in tailoring and cutting etc.

Qualifications and experience

Some employers require no formal qualifications and base their choice on the applicant's standard of education and personal qualities. Others prefer applicants to have GCSE passes (A–C) in English and maths.

Skilled machinists are constantly in demand, and for those who have been out of work for a while employers will often organise re-training to familiarise recruits with machines and working procedures. Most companies give applicants a practical aptitude test, together with a medical examination.

Other jobs

Window Dresser; Sales Assistant in clothing shop; Garment Examiner; Quality Controller; Alteration Hand

Contact

Write to CAPITB plc, 80 Richardshaw Lane, Pudsey, Leeds LS28 6BN; 0532 393355

Shelf Filler

Hours	Shift work available, often nights
Pay	£3 per hour; night shift work attracts extra allowances for unsocial hours
Personal qualities	Reliable; physically fit and strong; neat; pleasant; polite; able to work as member of a team

A shelf filler is employed to ensure that supermarket shelves are fully supplied with stock. She is responsible for watching stock levels, and bringing supplies in when they fall below a certain level; she prices items; wipes down dusty shelves and tins; she may cut up fresh produce, and, when required, assist customers.

Training is done on the job. Some large supermarkets

arrange an induction period for new staff, when they are told their duties by supervisors and are sometimes shown a short film on how the organisation operates.

Opportunities exist to progress and become section heads in charge of a number of shelf fillers. They can also change direction and work as sales assistants or checkout operators.

Qualifications and experience
No formal qualifications are required although most employers would expect applicants to have had a good standard of general education.

Other jobs
Checkout Operator; Mail Order Assembler; Counter Service Assistant; Petrol Pump Attendant; Merchandiser; Window Dresser

Contact
Your local supermarket to see if there are any vacancies

Social Worker

Hours	May work several days per week
Pay	Nationally agreed salaries for full-time social workers range from £11,241 increasing to £16,476 depending on experience and qualifications
Personal qualities	Compassionate; realistic; patient; emotionally stable; able to work as member of team or alone

A social worker offers advice and assistance to people facing social or personal problems.

Usually a field social worker will be assigned a number of clients including children at risk, families with problems, individuals with physical or mental handicap, teenagers in trouble, and may also be involved in fostering or adoption work. It is her job to assess each individual's case and determine the relevant course of action to help them, if necessary in consultation with a team or her supervisor. She must also monitor progress and write up case reports.

It is her responsibility to liaise with social workers in her team and other professionals, eg doctors and the police. With further experience many social workers specialise in areas such as medical social work or residential care.

Qualifications and experience
The professional qualification required by social workers is the Certificate of Qualification in Social Work (CQSW) and it is open to anyone irrespective of their age or qualifications.

Social work is an area which mature students are encouraged to enter, and there are some courses specifically designed for students over 30; courses are generally a combination of theory and practice.

The CQSW involves a two-year course for non-graduates under 25. Entry requirements are five GCSE passes (A-C) including English. There are also courses for those over 25.

The CQSW is gradually being replaced by the Diploma in Social Work (DipSW). The training lasts at least two years and the award is attainable at different levels: graduate, non-graduate, mature entrant.

Degree course students need two A levels and five GCSE passes (A-C). Consult college prospectuses for particular entry requirements.

The usual route is for trainees to undertake a three-year course. Graduates who have the relevant qualifications and experience may undertake a two-year course.

Other jobs
Youth and Community Worker; Nursery Nurse; Care Worker; Voluntary Work

Contact
Local council

Specialist publications in which vacancies appear: *Social Work Today; The Lady; Community Care; Community Action; City Limits; Time Out*

Write to: Central Council for Education and Training in Social Work (address on page 151)

Speech Therapist

Hours	Two to three days per week, depending on local health authority
Pay	Speech therapists' full-time wages rise by incremental points through grades A–E. The lowest salary grade A starts at £9500 and rises to around £18,500 at grade E
Personal qualities	Patient; sympathetic; tactful; clear voice; good hearing; decisive; well organised

A speech therapist is employed to assist people who are suffering from a speech, language or voice defect. She is responsible for the assessment, diagnosis and treatment of the patient. She does this by getting to know the patient, thereby gaining his or her confidence. She can then devise remedial programmes. A speech therapist works closely with children or adults who have speech problems caused by accidents or illness; she writes reports and monitors progress; attends case conferences and liaises with other professionals, ie doctors, teachers, social workers and psychologists.

A speech therapist may also find herself counselling members of the patient's family so that they understand the extent of the patient's disability and how they can offer support to aid recovery.

For fully experienced speech therapists there is always the possibility to move into teaching or research.

Qualifications and experience
Speech therapy is the type of profession that lends itself to career breaks. It is, however, important that knowledge of

current changes and practices is kept up to date, which can be done through refresher courses.

Many colleges relax entry requirements for mature students and take relevant experience into account. Entry to the profession is at a graduate level and the minimum academic requirements for a relevant degree course are five GCSE passes (A–C) with two A levels including English. Competition for training places is strong and successful applicants normally have more than the minimum qualifications.

In order to practise, a speech therapist must be a licentiate of the College of Speech Therapists. The two main methods of achieving this are by completing a recognised degree course (three-year ordinary degree or four-year honours degree); candidates who hold a degree in linguistics, psychology or similar subject can qualify by successfully completing a two-year post graduate diploma course in clinical and communication studies. Both courses combine theory and clinical practice. The subjects covered include linguistics, audiology, phonetics, anatomy, psychology, etc.

Once admitted as licentiates of the College of Speech Therapists, they may then seek employment as qualified speech therapists with any health authority.

Other jobs
Social Worker; Teacher

Contact
Write to: The College of Speech Therapists, 6 Lechmere Road, London NW2 5BU; 081-459 8521

Sports Coach

Hours	Variable; could be weekend work or several hours in the evening twice or three times a week
Pay	Work can be undertaken on a voluntary

basis. National governing bodies of sport employ coaches on contracts for fixed salaries. Salaries are low initially with bonuses for good results. There is a national agreed scale for coaches employed by local authorities. For the self-employed earnings relate to the number of students and at the level they teach

Personal qualities   Enjoys working with people; physically fit and healthy; enthusiastic; articulate; can offer encouragement and instil confidence in pupils; calm

Sport is a flourishing industry. Coaches, whether professional or unpaid volunteers, who would like to pass on their knowledge and expertise, are constantly in demand. For every sport there are potential high-fliers, wanting to learn skills.

Most coaches, unless employed by a professional association, have amateur status (they do not get paid for their services). This in no way reflects on their standards or expertise, but whatever their ability, it is important they educate their pupils in the professional steps they should take.

A coach must devise strategies for pupils to get the best out of particular activities.

Whether a coach works as professional or amateur she must adhere to the rules and regulations of the sport's controlling body.

Qualifications and experience
Physical fitness and ability is more important than formal qualifications. Most coaches have taken a recognised coaching qualification relevant to the sport they are teaching and this may be done on a part-time basis but requirements vary from sport to sport.

Other jobs
Youth and Community Work; Teacher; Swimming Pool Attendant; Leisure Pool Attendant

Contact
Local sports clubs

Write to: Information Centre, The Sports Council, 16 Upper Woburn Place, London WC1H 0QP; 071-388 1277

National Coaching Foundation, 4 College Close, Beckett Park, Leeds LS6 3QH; 0532 744802

Local Government Training Board, 4th Floor, The Arndale Centre, Luton, Bedfordshire LU1 2TS; 0582 451166

Swimming Pool Attendant

Hours	May be required to work unsocial hours involving evenings and/or weekends
Pay	£3–£5 per hour
Personal qualities	Good swimmer; knowledge of first aid; sociable; smart; physically strong; observant; able to cope in an emergency; able to work as member of team

A swimming pool attendant is usually employed to assist during the pool's opening hours. Naturally, tasks vary in different pools, but usually include: patrolling the pool area; administering lifeguard duties; offering first aid if required; and ensuring the safety of all pool users. Other duties may include mundane jobs such as cleaning the pool and the surrounding area, overseeing changing rooms and checking pool equipment.

A pool attendant must know how to undertake pool water tests and understand how the plant operates; it may be their responsibility also to carry out maintenance to the equipment as and when required.

The job may involve occasional work early in the morning

to make the pool ready, or helping at swimming events or weekends.

Depending on the size of the swimming pool, the attendant may work as one of a team.

Qualifications and experience
A good standard of general education is generally required by employers, but most important is that applicants should possess the relevant swimming qualifications which include: bronze medallion or pool lifeguard bronze medallion and a recognised first aid qualification.

Experience as a swimming instructor or lifeguard attendant would be beneficial.

Other jobs
Swimming Coach; Lifeguard Attendant; Leisure Pool Attendant

Contact
Local council; local swimming baths

Vacancies with local authorities are advertised in *Opportunities*; *Leisure Opportunities*

Tax Inspector

Hours	Several days per week
Pay	A full-time tax inspector is paid on a fixed scale from £10,135 to £16,242 depending on age, qualifications and experience
Personal qualities	High standard of spoken and written English; responsible; impartial; numerate; resilient; perceptive

A tax inspector is employed by the Inland Revenue. Her main job is to examine accounts appertaining to businesses, organisations and individuals to assess the amount of capital gains/income/corporation tax they are liable to pay. She does this, on occasions, by interviewing the client, and checking through their books, often discussing cases with accountants. She also advises clients on matters relating to tax and business law and, when the situation arises, represents the Crown.

Qualifications and experience
Opportunities exist for anyone wishing to return to any area of the Civil Service.

A first or second class honours degree or equivalent are the qualifications required to train as a tax inspector. To gain entry on to The Inspector of Taxes Graduate Entry Scheme applicants are required to be aged under 36 years. The selection process is by an initial interview followed by two days of written and oral examinations.

Training to be a tax inspector is a lengthy and intensive course, divided into two parts. The first part introduces the trainee tax inspector into the world of business and business accounts; the second part covers law and company accounts. The training courses take place in London and several other centres around the country. After the end of the first introductory three-year course in which trainees find out all about accounts and business law they are expected to attend regular courses throughout their career.

Newly qualified tax inspectors usually serve a two-year probationary period and if they have failed the Part 1 written examination may find the probationary period will be extended.

Other jobs
Accounting Technician; Bank Cashier

Contact
Write to: Civil Service Commission, Alencon Link, Basingstoke, Hampshire RG21 1JB; 0256 846560

Tea Lady

Hours	Variable – may be 9.30am–4.00pm
Pay	Variable
Personal qualities	Pleasant; clean; reliable; able to make a good cup of tea

In many offices and factories the automatic vending machine which produces piping hot cups of tea, coffee or hot chocolate in a matter of seconds has revolutionised catering and made the conventional tea lady redundant. However, in firms which have not yet automated, opportunities still exist for a tea lady.

Her main job is making the tea/coffee, and then laying up her trolley with cups and saucers and alternative beverages; she may also offer a selection of snacks. Once the tea has been served she returns later to collect the dirty dishes and then washes them up. The same ritual is carried out again in the afternoon. Occasionally her duties may overlap with assisting other kitchen staff at lunchtime in the canteen.

Overall, a pleasant job for someone who enjoys meeting people.

Qualifications and experience
No formal qualifications are required to be a tea lady. Personal qualities are far more important.

Other jobs
Kitchen Assistant; Counter Assistant; Cook; Midday Supervisor

Contact
Job vacancy boards outside firms

Telephone Salesperson

Hours	Approximately 15 hours per week
Pay	£3.50 per hour plus bonus
Personal qualities	Clear voice; good hearing; polite; self-confident; determined; persuasive; pleasant; calm

Telephone sales people obtain orders for goods or services by telephoning customers (telesales). Duties include: taking orders and, using catalogues or a computer to check on the availability and price of the required item, possibly encouraging an alternative choice if the initial one is not available, and ensuring that the goods are despatched. Advertising (space selling) is often handled by this means.

The sales sometimes involve expensive installations such as fitted kitchens, fitted bedrooms or double glazing.

She has to keep records of sales, together with customer information, and she may find herself occasionally dealing with complaints from members of the public. On-the-job training will be given.

Qualifications and experience
No formal qualifications are required but employers expect their staff to have a good standard of general education with some GCSE passes (A–C) including English and maths.

Someone with experience in selling or telephone work could find this an interesting job. It is demanding and tiring and some people find it hard to accept rejections.

Other jobs
Sales Representative; Telephonist

Telephonist

Hours	Approximately 15–20 hrs per week
Pay	£3 per hour
Personal qualities	Clear voice; good hearing; tactful; calm; patient; good concentration; able to work alone; polite

A telephonist operates a switchboard. She connects callers by pushing plugs or removing keys when lights on the switchboard are illuminated. She also dials numbers for callers who are having difficulty in connecting with their destination. If employed by British Telecom a telephonist will usually be responsible for answering direct enquiries, taking details of any reported faults, and also dealing with emergency 999 calls.

In a small organisation reception duties may also be part of the telephonist's work.

Training is generally done on the job under the supervision of qualified staff.

In time and with experience a telephonist could become a supervisor or move into other areas of office work.

Qualifications and experience
Although personal attributes are very important in such a job, employers still expect staff to have a good standard of general education with preferably some GCSE passes (A–C) including English.

Other jobs
Night Desk Clerk; Clerk; Receptionist

Temporary Work

Hours	Temporary work may involve filling in for someone on maternity or sick leave; or working sporadically via one of the many agencies
Pay	From £3 per hour
Personal qualities	Pleasant; sociable; adaptable; smart; able to get on with people; able to drive an advantage; reliable

Throughout the year but especially during holidays vacancies arise for temporary staff. Such opportunities crop up in many areas of work: offices, shops, hospitals, farms (fruit and potato picking), factory work etc. Many employers advertise vacancies in the newspapers but there are numerous agencies which actually have a permanent register of employers seeking temporary staff.

Employers expect staff to be fully trained.

Temping is very flexible, offering the opportunity to earn a wage without feeling tied down, and can help someone to gain experience. Furthermore, it offers the opportunity of meeting people. It is a good way to prepare for a return to full-time work.

Qualifications and experience
Qualifications and experience relate to the particular type of area in which employment is being sought and these will be established at the initial interview with the employer/agency. Usually agencies set applicants a short test to establish their level of ability.

Other jobs
Voluntary Work

Contact
Temporary agencies

135

Toy Library Organiser

Hours	Variable – perhaps one to two hours per week
Pay	Usually none, unless it is sponsored by local authority
Personal qualities	Expert in dealing with the under fives; knowledge of fundraising; able to organise and delegate; patient

The basic idea of a toy library is to enable young children to enjoy a wider variety of toys than they have at home.

Toy libraries also fulfil other equally important needs within the community: offering both support and friendship to those families who need social contact; a place where social workers and parents alike can meet and talk without feeling under pressure from outside sources; and they also offer the opportunity for children to play with others.

The child goes along to the toy library and, for a small fee, borrows a toy which can then be taken home for a week or so. Naturally, if the toy gets broken or lost there is a fine (it may be 50p), but such a system possibly teaches young children to respect other people's property.

Although it is usual for toy libraries to be run by professional health visitors or playgroup leaders, for example, there is a growing awareness of their usefulness which has prompted many others to join forces and form their own. They may hire the local church hall or community centre once a week, but buses have been converted into mobile toy libraries travelling to densely populated housing estates or outlying rural districts.

Organising a toy library can be enormous fun. Obviously, a great deal of preparation needs to be done: finding the premises, acquiring a selection of toys; calculating the costs (consider that there will be broken toys to repair), and also co-ordinating the work of other volunteers.

Most inner cities have at least one toy library, but they range from highly organised schemes to those run on a shoestring. While some receive backing from local authority grants, the great majority have to rely on donations and survive by raising money through jumble sales, sponsored events, or coffee mornings.

Qualifications and experience
No formal qualifications are required to set up and organise a toy library but experience in a similar venture would be advantageous.

Other jobs
Playgroup Helper; Auxiliary Assistant; Nanny

Contact
Chat with the local Social Services Department to see if they are prepared to subsidise such a project; read books on fundraising activities

Translator

Hours	Freelance translators work hours to suit themselves – subject to client's requirements
Pay	Regular full-time employees can earn from £10,000
Personal qualities	Knowledge of at least one foreign language; self-motivated; reliable; accurate; quick; creative

Translators are employed to translate from their mother tongue into another language (and vice versa) reports, letters, manuals, and contracts. The script must be translated as though it were written in that language initially.

Such translation work may be separated into two main types, technical-scientific and literary. Both require great expertise, although it appears there is less demand for the latter.

As there is normally a deadline for delivery of the material to be translated, it is important that the translator works very quickly.

Most translators work on a freelance basis and find employment through agencies. The best way to find an agency in your area is via Yellow Pages or library and information office. Because the work is not regular, most translators have other employment.

The areas in which part-time opportunities exist for translators are: industry and commerce; the Civil Service; the BBC; translation bureaux and agencies.

Qualifications and experience

Age is irrelevant; the ability to speak fluently in several languages is deemed far more important. This is often only achieved after years of gaining knowledge and experience.

The main qualification required for a translator is a complete knowledge of at least one foreign language and a good command of the English language; it is also useful to have specialist knowledge in some particular field. Organisations differ as regards their entry requirements; usually they expect applicants to be able to translate several languages both ways, and to possess a degree in languages. It is useful to be able to type.

The Institute of Linguists offers examinations in translating and covers GCSE to degree level. Both the certificates and diplomas are widely accepted by employers. Courses are organised through college evening classes or the National Extension College.

Contact

Agencies (names may be found in local Yellow Pages)

The Institute of Linguists, 24A Highbury Grove, London N5 2EA; 071-359 7445

Write to: Institute of Translation & Interpreting, 318A Finchley Road, London NW3 5HT; 071-794 9931

Usherette

Hours	Evening or afternoon sessions
Pay	£3-£5 per hour
Personal qualities	Sociable; smart; good eyesight; helpful; courteous

An usherette may be employed in a cinema or theatre. Before allowing visitors into the auditorium she will check that their tickets correspond with the film showing before directing them to their seats.

An usherette may combine her role with that of cashier; taking payment at the kiosk from patrons and when required, serving at the refreshment desk; she may also go into the cinema and serve ice creams during the interval.

During the performance she must maintain a watchful eye and ask anyone causing a disturbance to leave. She must also ensure the alleyways are kept clear at all times in case of an emergency. Usually training is given on the job.

Qualifications and experience
Personal attributes are more important than formal qualifications but most employers expect staff to have a good standard of general education.

This kind of job often involves working unsocial hours with the probability of weekend work too. However, it can suit a busy housewife who finds herself able to work only in the evenings.

Other jobs
Receptionist; Waitress; Counter Assistant

Contact
The local cinema

Veterinary Nurse

Hours	Part-time hours may be possible in a small veterinary practice which is open once or twice a week
Pay	Pay is low whether or not the nurses possess the recognised qualifications. Full-timers earn from £5600 to around £13,000
Personal qualities	Dedicated; calm; animal lover; not squeamish; patient; reassuring; physically fit; able to work alone

A veterinary nurse works alongside the veterinary surgeon in the treatment and care of the animals. Her responsibilities include: assisting in the operating theatre; sterilising instruments, preparing any medication required, collecting specimens and on occasion taking X-rays. Before and during operations she stays with the animal checking monitors and anaesthetic, and handing over instruments as and when needed. She also looks after the animals during their recovery.

A veterinary nurse is responsible for ensuring that the surgery is kept spotlessly clean and she may occasionally take over reception duties, maintain records, deal with correspondence etc.

A knowledge of animal first aid is also useful so that she is able to deal with emergencies when the vet is out on call.

Qualifications and experience
Although there is no age limit for this work, applicants without qualifications may find it difficult to gain employment.

To study for the Royal College Veterinary Surgeon scheme and become a qualified veterinary nurse candidates must have at least four GCSE passes (A–C) including English language and a physical or biological science or maths. They must also find employment at an Approved Training Centre before enrolling for the scheme. Contact the Royal College of

Veterinary Surgeons, 32 Belgrave Square, London SW1X 8QP; 071-235 4971 for a list of centres, enclosing an SAE.

Other jobs
Dog Beautician; Dog Walker

Contact
Local vets to see if they require anyone to assist

Veterinary Record; Veterinary Nursing Journal, available from the secretary of the British Veterinary Nursing Association, Seedbed Centre, Coldharbour Road, Harlow, Essex CM19 5AF; 0279 450567

Voluntary Work

Hours	Whatever time the individual is able to dedicate to it
Pay	Usually none
Personal qualities	Patient; reliable; pleasant; enthusiastic; physically fit; tolerant; sympathetic; able to get on with people

Voluntary work covers a wide spectrum of opportunities: working with physically and/or mentally handicapped people; delivering meals on wheels; working in a charity shop; helping at a rehabilitation centre; talking to the elderly at a day centre; assisting in a local children's playgroup; befriending someone in prison and visiting them whenever time allows; helping in a political campaign; working as a Samaritan; offering support to victims of crime – it really depends upon the amount of time you have available and are willing to dedicate.

Volunteer workers come from all walks of life: professional people, housewives, retired people, people who have recovered from serious illnesses and wish to express gratitude.

Depending on which area you decide to work, training on the job is usually done under the supervision of experienced staff.

Voluntary work can offer people so very much: an opportunity to meet and make new friends; a break from the daily routine; it also builds up one's confidence and in many cases is a stepping stone to a new job. In fact, many community and social workers begin their career working on a voluntary basis, before taking a specialised course.

Qualifications and experience
No formal qualifications are required to be a voluntary worker. Personal attributes are far more important.

Other jobs
Social Worker; Youth and Community Worker; Care Worker

Contact
Local Social Services Department; local library for details of voluntary groups in your area

Write to: Community Service Volunteers (The National Volunteer Agency), 237 Pentonville Road, London N1 9JN; 071-278 6601

The National Council for Voluntary Organisations, 26 Bedford Square, London WC1B 3HU; 071-636 4066

Voluntary Advisory Service, London Voluntary Council, 68 Charlton Street, London NW1 1JR; 071-388 0241

Waitress

Hours	Various opportunities to work on temporary or casual basis at weekends, or shift work. Hours according to employer's requirements
Pay	Minimum rate £2.33 per hour

| Personal qualities | Pleasant; neat; polite; alert; physically fit; clear voice; good memory; quick |

A waitress is employed to serve food at dining tables in restaurants and hotels. She takes the customers' orders and relays them to the kitchen.

Work varies between different restaurants. In some formal restaurants a waitress serves food at the diner's table (silver service), while in others meals are delivered to the customer ready on plates.

Her other duties involve preparing bills, taking payment, giving out change, clearing and laying the table in readiness for the next customer.

Training is generally undertaken on the job, and is supervised by an experienced member of staff. Occasionally there are practice sessions before or after opening hours. Many establishments run extra training courses which deal with general subjects such as fire prevention or health and safety. Some waitresses may wish to specialise in a particular area, such as wine-waiting (when they are known also as sommeliers) and are able to take a specialist examination set by the Guild of Sommeliers to qualify as a Master Sommelier.

Qualifications and experience
Most employers expect staff to have had a good standard of general education and to possess some GCSE passes (A–C). Mature applicants are looked upon favourably, especially those with experience in the catering or hotel industry.

A variety of courses is available. Many technical colleges run one- or two-year courses leading to the City and Guilds 707 Certificate in Food and Beverage Service. Part 1 of the course (707-1) offers an introduction to the hotel and catering industry, teaching the knowledge and skills required for such waiting work. The subjects studied include food and beverage, dealing with customers, working with fellow staff and communications etc. Those successfully completing the course are able to work in any type of food service. Additional experience may be necessary before the full range of waitressing duties can be performed.

Students who have successfully completed Part 1 and had some experience in the catering industry can sit for the Food and Beverage Part 2 courses (707-2) in which more advanced serving techniques, including the preparation of food at trolleys, catering at functions, merchandising and social skills are taught.

Other jobs
Bar Staff; Counter Service Assistant; Kitchen Assistant; Midday Supervisor; Cook

Contact
Write to: Hotel and Catering Training Company, International House, High Street, Ealing, London W5 5DB; 081-579 2400

Hotel and Catering Trades Job Centre, 1–3 Denmark Street, London WC2H 8LR; 071-497 2047

Window Cleaner

Hours	Largely depend on the weather
Pay	Based on the number of windows cleaned. Window cleaning rates vary between regions from £1 to £30 per house or flat
Personal qualities	Physically fit and strong; reliable; honest; a head for heights; enjoys working alone; able to drive an advantage

Window cleaning may not appeal to all women but will pay handsome rewards for anyone who enjoys working outdoors. Large factories and schools employ their own contract cleaners, but the householder has problems finding a good reliable window cleaner and this is where a self-employed person could provide an invaluable service.

Although the job entails working outside in all weathers the hours can be flexible and made to fit round domestic responsibilities. It may be desirable to work at the weekend when there is someone available to take care of the family, or alternatively a few hours during the day. If the work is done in the householder's absence, it is necessary to call back for payment.

Qualifications and experience
Although window cleaning may be a physically demanding job it is quite possible for women to do it; they can even reduce the workload by taking on a partner.

The ability to drive is an advantage and, better still, if you can buy an old van to transport ladders and other equipment round in.

If the idea of becoming a self-employed window cleaner sounds appealing then set about doing it in a businesslike fashion. Chat with window cleaners in other areas (they won't welcome rivals) and find out how they began their business; make an appointment with the manager at the local small business unit and possibly the bank who will be able to give financial advice.

Other jobs
Home Help; Cleaner; School Crossing Patrol

Contact
Place advertisements in local shop windows or newspapers

Potential customers may be found in your locality; inform them of your service by having cards printed and distributed

Window Dresser

Hours	Many are employed on a freelance basis
Pay	Payment is related to experience. A full-time window dresser with the relevant qualifications can expect to earn £112 per week

Personal qualities   Artistic flair; tidy; nimble fingered;
physically fit; good colour sense; adaptable;
able to work alone or as part of team

A window dresser is generally employed in retail shops. She is responsible for displaying goods in the shop window to attract the attention of the public, and inside the store.

She arranges displays, working from her own designs or from drawings. She must collect together all the materials necessary to create an eye-catching display and assemble them using dummies, paint, thread, pins, paper etc; sometimes she must press clothes and organise price tickets. She must ensure that the display is kept clean and occasionally she may be asked to assist in the shop.

Before gaining employment it is usual for window display staff to complete a full-time course and gain the relevant qualifications.

Qualifications and experience
Although there are no schemes specifically geared to mature entrants it is possible to get employment as a sales assistant first and then make a sideways move. Alternatively, one can follow a training programme.

To gain entry on to a course most colleges require applicants to have four GCSE passes (A–C) including art and English. It is quite usual for those receiving in-store training to obtain qualifications on a day release basis. The two examining bodies which offer courses in display are the British Display Society (BDS) and the Business and Technician Education Council (BTEC).

The BDS General Certificate Grade I is a one-year full-time course – no educational qualifications are required. It can be followed by the BDS General Certificate Grade II. The BDS National Diploma (Advanced Level) is a two-year full-time course for which applicants must have three GCSE passes (A–C) including art and English. The BDS National Diploma (Final Level) is a one-year full-time course for holders of the advanced level or a BTEC diploma. This course offers the opportunity to specialise in display or point-of-sale design.

The BDS Technician Certificate course is a part-time course and studied in three stages. Preliminary/I, Intermediate/II and Final/III. No educational qualifications are needed; however, a portfolio of work should be taken along to the interview. The BTEC (Board of Design) courses include the National Certificate in Display and Exhibition Design, a full-time course for which the entry requirement is 3 GCSE passes (A–C); the National Certificate in Design (Display), a part-time course run at the Isle of Ely College (East Anglia) and Hugh Baird College of Further Education (Bootle). Entry qualifications are three GCSE passes (A–C), and art or a related subject may be required; the National Diploma in Design (Display) is a full-time course which requires applicants to have three GCSE passes (A–C).

Other jobs
Store Demonstrator; Shelf Filler; Merchandiser; Retail Assistant; Receptionist; Cashier; Checkout Operator

Contact
Write to: Business and Technician Education Council, Central House, Upper Woburn Place, London WC1H 0HH; 071-388 3288

British Display Society, Guardian House 92–94 Foxberry Road, London SE4 2SH; 081-692 8943

Word Processor Operator

Hours	10-20 hours per week
Pay	£3.75-£4 per hour
Personal qualities	Methodical; quick; neat; alert; good concentration; able to carry out instructions; able to work as member of team

147

A word process operator is responsible for operating the machine which basically consists of a keyboard, a screen on which she can see what she is typing, a systems unit, and a printer which prints out the final copy when it is ready. The keyboard is that of the conventional typewriter, plus extra instruction keys for deleting, inserting, recalling copy that has already been produced, 'finding' copy that has been stored, and for printing out the number of copies required. Corrections, alterations and additions are made by 'calling up' on the screen the relevant line or page and then correcting the text by pressing the relevant keys. Headings can be centred or ranged left at the touch of a key.

The machine can produce personalised letters by merging text already stored with a file of names and addresses held in its memory. The memory can be used as a filing system and reduces the need for paper files. Selected information can be withdrawn from the memory store. There are spell-checking programmes which will pick out words not in the memory, so the operator can confirm the correct spelling.

Training in operating word processors is often provided by the employer or by the supplier of the equipment, either in the office or at a centre. Adult education centres, secretarial colleges and agencies also run courses.

Qualifications and experience
A good standard of general education is required by most employers together with some GCSE passes (A–C) including maths and English. The ability to type must precede a word processing course to get the best results.

Other jobs
Audio Typist; Copy Typist

Contact
Employment agencies for temporary work

Youth and Community Worker

Hours	Could involve a morning, afternoon or evening session
Pay	Approximately £14.25 per session
Personal qualities	Reliable; understanding; resilient; physically strong; tactful; sense of humour; outgoing personality

Local authority and voluntary organisations employ youth and community workers in the many clubs, centres and other such venues where people meet.

Her duties include: organising social, sporting or educational activities for the community such as judo, craft workshops, discos and outdoor activities; offering support and counselling to those who need it, and also giving information and acting as a link between youngsters and the experts.

Although most youth and community workers are employed by local authority education departments and social services departments a great many find employment working for Scout and Girl Guides associations, boys' clubs, church and local organisations.

Qualifications and experience
To qualify as a youth and community worker students must either undertake a recognised diploma/certificate course of initial training or a postgraduate course.

Many of the courses for youth and community work are for late entrants, the average age being 27, and in some circumstances employers waive academic qualifications for someone who has had experience in such work.

To be accepted on to a course in youth and community work applicants should meet the following requirements: (a) be at least twenty-three years of age; (b) possess five GCSE passes (A–C) (there may be an exception for a mature applicant or someone with previous experience in youth and community work either on a part-time or voluntary basis).

Each year there are around 250 places available on two-year courses which are endorsed by the Council for Education and Training in Youth and Community Work. Although these courses vary in content most of them include: social history and policy, welfare rights, human development, administration and management relationship skills and a great amount of supervised field placements. For information on training courses write to the Council for Education and Training in Youth and Community Work (address below).

All newly qualified youth and community workers are required to serve a supervised probationary year before being registered as fully qualified workers.

Other jobs
Sports Coach; Voluntary Worker; Care Assistant

Contacts
Local Youth Clubs; Church organisations

Write to: Council for Education and Training in Youth and Community Work, Wellington House, Wellington Street, Leicester LE1 6HL; 0533 555666

Joint Negotiating Committee for Youth and Community Workers, Staff Panel, Hamilton House, Mabledon Place, London WC1H 9BD; 071-388 6191

National Council of YMCAs, 640 Forest Road, Walthamstow, London E17 3DZ; 081-520 5599

Youth Clubs UK, Keswick House, 30 Peacock Lane, Leicester LE1 5NY; 0533 29514

Useful Addresses

Business and Technician Education Council (BTEC)
Central House, Upper Woburn Square, London WC1H 0HH;
071-388 3288

Central Council for Education and Training in Social Work
England: CCETSW Information Service, Derbyshire House,
St Chad's Street, London WC1H 8AD; 071-278 2455

Northern Ireland: CCETSW Information Service, Malone
Road, Belfast BT9 5BN; 0232 665390

Scotland: CCETSW Information Service, 78–80 George
Street, Edinburgh EH2 3BU; 031-220 0093

Wales: CCETSW Information Service, West Wing, St David's
House, Wood Street, Cardiff CF1 1ES; 0222 226257

City and Guilds of London Institute (C&G)
76 Portland Place, London W1N 4AA; 071-278 2468

National Extension College
18 Brooklands Avenue, Cambridge CB2 2HN; 0223 316644

Nursing
**English National Board for Nursing, Midwifery and
Health Visiting**
Resource and Careers Service, PO Box 356, Sheffield S8 0SJ

**National Board for Nursing, Midwifery and Health
Visiting for Northern Ireland**
RAC House, 79 Chichester Street, Belfast BT1 4JR

The Nursing Adviser
Scottish Health Service Centre
Crewe Road, Edinburgh EH4 2LF

The Chief Nursing Officer
Welsh Office
Cathays Park, Cardiff CF1 3NG

Part Time Careers Ltd
10 Golden Square, London W1R 3AF; 071-437 3103/734 0559
An employment agency for part-time work in London; offers
advice and guidance

Scottish Vocational Education Council (SCOTVEC)
24 Douglas Street, Glasgow G2 7NG; 041-248 7900

Women Returners' Network
Secretary: Margaret Johnson
Garden Cottage
Youngsbury
Ware
Hertfordshire SG12 0TZ
Publishes a directory of education and training for women,
Returning to Work

Further Reading from Kogan Page

Getting There: Job Hunting for Women, 2nd edition, Margaret Wallis, 1990

Great Answers to Tough Interview Questions: How to Get the Job You Want, 2nd edition, Martin John Yate, 1989

How to Get a Job After 45, Julie Bayley, 1990

How to Survive as a Working Mother, Judith Steiner, 1989

Job Sharing: A Practical Guide, Pam Walton, 1990

Nursing as a Second Career, Margaret Korving, 1990

Returning to Work: A Practical Guide for Women, Alec Reed, 1989

Returning to Work, The Women Returners' Network, 1990

Test Your Own Aptitude, 2nd edition, Jim Barrett and Geoff Williams, 1990

Working for Yourself: The Daily Telegraph Guide to Self-Employment, Godfrey Golzen, (annual)

The Kogan Page Careers Series
This series consists of short guides (96–160 pages) to different careers for school and college leavers, graduates and anyone wanting to start anew. Each book serves as an introduction to a particular career and to jobs available within that field, including full details of training qualifications and courses. A list is available from the address on page 4 (facing Contents).